Violet Fane

Anthony Babington

A drama

Violet Fane

Anthony Babington
A drama

ISBN/EAN: 9783337303983

Printed in Europe, USA, Canada, Australia, Japan

Cover: Foto ©Thomas Meinert / pixelio.de

More available books at **www.hansebooks.com**

ANTHONY BABINGTON

A DRAMA

BY

VIOLET FANE

AUTHOR OF "DENZIL PLACE," "THE QUEEN OF THE FAIRIES." ETC.

LONDON
CHAPMAN AND HALL, 193, PICCADILLY
1877

IT is exactly two hundred and ninety years ago since most of the personages of whom mention is here made, suffered death upon a well-established charge of High Treason. If I have not represented Babington as being altogether a hero, it is, that a careful study of what is left for us to study, in his character, has seemed to justify to myself the view I have taken of it, and of the varying impulses which led him to associate himself with the religious politics of his day, and to give his countenance to the commission of a murder which appeared to himself and his partisans as an Act of Faith. Alice and Willoughby are merely imaginary characters, for though there is no reason why Jerome Bellamy should not have had a niece, I do not find any mention of one. The kinship here supposed to exist between this family and that of Babington is also imagined, as is Babington's interview with the

Queen of Scots at Tutbury, with whom, though he had so warmly embraced her cause, he never came in personal contact after her removal from Sheffield. But with these exceptions, this, my first Play, has, perhaps (amongst many others), the defect of being "a mere slice of history," and unfitted in form for the stage, even cóuld an audience be found patient enough to sit out so tragic a tragedy. However, "Let me be a warning to all young gentlemen, especially *generosis adolescentulis*," said Chidiock Titchborne in his last address to the populace; and though ambition, enthusiasm, and religious zeal may not be at this present the besetting sins of many of our "youths of generous blood," there may still lurk some moral in the contemplation, from afar off, of the errors for which these unfortunate young men paid, on this day,* so dearly, even though there may be some who will exclaim, in the words of Babington— "*Quorsum hæc alio properantibus?*" †

V. F.

* *20th Sept.*

† "What are these things to men hastening to another purpose?"—(*Written by Babington under the picture of himself and his companions.*)

"My prime of youth is but a frost of cares,
   My feast of joy is but a dish of pain,
   My crop of corn is but a field of tares,
   And all my goodes is but vain hope of gain.
The day is fled, and yet I saw no sun,
And now I live, and now my life is done!

"My spring is past, and yet it hath not sprung,
   The fruit is dead and yet the leaves are green,
   My youth is past, and yet I am but young,
   I saw the world and yet I was not seen;
My thread is cut and yet it is not spun,
And now I live, and now my life is done!"

(Verses made by Chidiock Titchborne of himselfe in the Tower the night before he suffered death, who was executed for treason, 1586.)

DRAMATIS PERSONÆ.

ANTHONY BABINGTON (a Catholic Gentleman of Derbyshire).

QUEEN ELIZABETH.

MARY QUEEN OF SCOTS.

SIR WILLIAM CECIL (Lord Burghley, Lord Treasurer).

SIR FRANCIS WALSINGHAM (one of the principal secre-
taries'of the Queen of England).

EARL OF LEICESTER (Master of the Horse).

SIR CHRISTOPHER HATTON (Vice-Chamberlain).

EARL OF SHREWSBURY (Earl Marshal of England and
keeper of the Queen of Scots).

MARY BEATON (in waiting on the Queen of Scots).

MRS. BELLAMY.

JEROME BELLAMY (her Son).

ALICE BELLAMY (her Granddaughter).

MRS. BABINGTON.

COLONEL NICHOLAS WILLOUGHBY.

JOHN BALLARD (a Jesuit).

ROBERT BARNWELL (an Irish Gentleman).

THOMAS SALISBURY.

CHARLES TILNEY.

JOHN SAVAGE.

HENRY DONN.

CHIDIOCK TITCHBORNE (a Hampshire Gentleman).

THOMAS GERRARD.

EDWARD WINDSOR.

JOHN CHARNOCK, &c.

} Conspirators.

PETER BARTON (servant to Babington).

FATHER HARINGTON (a Priest).

GILES (servant to the Bellamys). .

Courtiers, Lords, Citizens, Landlord of "Three Tuns," a Child, Soldiers, Jailers, Servants, Pages, &c. &c.

ANTHONY BABINGTON.

ACT I.

Scene I.—*An inner room at the tavern of the " Three Tuns," in Newgate Market;* Anthony Babington, *seated at a table, shrouded in a cloak and disguised as an old man, with false beard, surrounded by nine of his Fellow-conspirators.* John Ballard, *also disguised, and under the name of " Captain Fortescue."* Peter Barton, *a servant of* Babington's. *Tankards, flagons, and remains of a supper.*

BALLARD.

We must call for another flagon of wine, so that they deem we meet here only to drink. [*Calls for wine, which is brought.*] Are we all assembled?

B

BABINGTON.

One is wanting, but he will be here anon.

BALLARD.

See that the doors are locked [*doors secured*] while I read over the names of those present. Anthony Babington, of Dethwick (under God the prime mover in this good cause), John Charnock, Edward Windsor, Thomas Salisbury, Robert Barnwell, Thomas Gerrard, John Savage, Charles Tilney, Henry Donn, and myself, John Ballard, a priest of the most holy Order of Jesus; but who will be known and addressed this evening as Captain Fortescue, a soldier of fortune.

CONSPIRATORS.

We are all here, save Mr. Chidiock Titchborne, of South Hants, whom we are momentarily expecting.

BALLARD.

Now I would have you all to say once more that ye be agreed in this undertaking, which is for the ultimate good of all Christendom; for though you have each one partaken of the blessed sacrament, swearing thereon to be united together to this end, I

would have him that fears for his life to withdraw
from the midst of us, lest his ensample should cause
others to falter.

CONSPIRATORS.

We are all agreed.

BALLARD.

Then we may hope for great things. Ye have
heard how the Holy Father, Christ's vicar on earth,
hath graciously extended unto him that shall be the
chosen instrument of God, his absolution and his
blessing ; seeing that in ridding the world of the Beast,
great glory must needs accrue to the one true faith ?

CONSPIRATORS.

We have heard the gracious message of his
Holiness.

BALLARD.

You, John Savage, have good reason to rejoice,
in that you have been specially singled out and pre-
destined of heaven to accomplish this great work.
Sometime a soldier under his most catholic highness
the Prince of Parma, may you find yourself ere long
enrolled amongst the glorious army of Christ's saints,
in whose service if so be that you endure martyrdom,

B 2

all the more will you be assured of your eternal reward.

JOHN SAVAGE.

Amen !

BALLARD.

Yet it is an old saying, and one to be reverenced, that two heads are better than one ; and so with the hands that are to strike—they should be ready on all sides—let them but bide their time. For we should not let the weight of so mighty an undertaking depend alone on the finite prowess of one man. You, Robert Barnwell, in that you are an inmate at this present of the Court, and Charles Tilney, seeing that you are one of the pensioners of the heretic queen (whom we speak of as the Beast that doth trouble Christendom), and therefore one of those last to be suspected, you will have access in many ways to the royal presence, denied to others amongst us, who would, nevertheless, rejoice at the same chance, whereof see that ye profit, and that ye strike home.

CONSPIRATORS.

We bide our time.

BALLARD.

This is the way we hope to work for God. Firstly, we propose to remove the Beast that troubles the earth; and when this great good is achieved, then shall we strike at the hearts of all those her evil counsellors who have confirmed and strengthened her in her evil course. Cecil, Walsingham, Francis Knollys, and Hunsdon—these are the names of those to be doomed and damned. May their deaths serve as a warning to all such as militate against Christ's kingdom on earth.

CONSPIRATORS.

Amen !

BALLARD.

Once again, have ye given up, all of you, the safest and surest way of dealing with her whose living is a curse? I have in my mind her removal by poison, to be administered in her food by those of her creatures whom we may convert for the glory of God.

BABINGTON.

As English gentlemen, this is an idea not to be entertained by us.

BALLARD.

I spoke of it but as a method which would not be fraught with the same dangers that must needs now lurk in your path; the tortures inflicted on the blessed Balthasar Gerard, the instrument of heaven who so bravely freed the world of the heretic Prince of Orange, affright you not?

BABINGTON.

What a French lad, base born, could dare and endure, are we, who are Englishmen, to shrink from?

BALLARD.

Then we are all agreed?

BABINGTON.

Mr. Titchborne is for some safe middle course. He hath said to me more than once of this project: "So it involved not the killing of a woman, and she my queen, I would join to you with the more zeal."

BALLARD.

He that is minded to croak, or to clap a wet clout on our endeavours, let him cry off.

[*Knock at door.*

LANDLORD.

A gentleman of your party who has been delayed.

[*Enter* CHIDIOCK TITCHBORNE.]

TITCHBORNE.

Good evening, friends. A cold March after our green Yule.

BABINGTON.

" A green Yule makes a full kirkyard," as the Scots say.

TITCHBORNE.

It was heavy travelling over the Hampshire moors. But our farmers say of the cold, Better now than later.

BALLARD.

God prosper the harvest. [*Exit* LANDLORD.] But he is departed now, so a truce to the weather and the crops. Though, now I bethink me, your greeting, Babington, would not make a bad password, for a time at least; though we must change it to another ere long, for safety. It were well that those gentlemen who are joined together in this great cause should have some string of words by

the introducing of which into their careless talk
they may make known which way lie their sym-
pathies; for each day the circle of those who work
for the glory of God will wax larger, and there may
be those amongst us in a week who to-day know
not where to turn for comfort.   Let it be told to
our friends that with this greeting they may be sure
of a welcome: "A green Yule maketh a full kirkyard," in some method interpolated into their talk;
and lest it should be said lightly and by accident
by those who are ignorant of its significance, let
them afterwards say, in carelesswise, "God prosper
the harvest."   You have made a note of this, gentlemen?

CONSPIRATORS.

We have.

PETER BARTON.

I am no scholar; would one of these gentlemen
write the words?   [BABINGTON *writes.*

BALLARD (*to* TITCHBORNE).

And now, sir, how comes this, and you a Catholic
gentleman, one of the good old stock?   How so
luke-minded?   For I hear that you shrink from what

must needs be our crowning good. There is an apathy as damnable 'fore God as evil deeds. Buckle yourself for action !

BABINGTON.

Bear with him, father, he is with us privily ; but, like myself, he hath a wife. He plays a game of hazard most disastrous if he lose. Her heart breaks with his neck.

BALLARD (*aside*).

Hush, Babington ! your words unnerve him. And of your own wife, how often have you said that she stood not in your way?

TITCHBORNE.

It is as you say. I wish you well. Yet well I also wish others had worked for this—not my true friends. See, too, your idol be not made of clay— the lady of your dreams. I say no more, fearing to anger you ; but since seeing you I have had more proof of the truth of those grievous reports—the rumours of her evil living heretofore.

BALLARD.

There is no purity that can withstand
Obliquity of vision. As I watch'd

From this gray square of window, waiting you,
Before the daylight vanish'd, I beheld
The very snowflakes, on their earthward side,
Look black against the whiter space of sky,
Yet were they very part of that same world
Of unshed purity.   Be generous,
You do not know her ; your material eyes
See but the under-shadow cast by earth
Upon the falling snowflakes.

TITCHBORNE.
                    Yet, my friends, .
Be ye not trick'd by vain ambitions.   Anthony,
There are good things besides the love of fame
And smiles of princes.   I am not long wed
To one who makes the world seem emptiness
And home a world of blessings.   Politics
Involve in these our days such tortuous
Deceptions, such false dealings, all for ends
So fork'd and complicated, budding forth
In doubtful double-blossom—France and Spain,
Poor Ireland, where the ragged rightful lords
Wait, like a grisly pack of famish'd wolves,
To spring on their oppressors.   Add to this,

Cold Scotland, too, and Flanders ; 'tis a match
Flung in a mine of powder, this same plot
To crown the Scottish Mary.   Mark my words !
The queen is such a weathercock to turn
That what she wills to-day is but a sign
She change her mood to-morrow ; she may yet
Name Mary Stuart her heir.   And one thing more—
I would that ye could keep from deed of blood—
You guess my thought—think of it, Anthony—
A woman and your queen !   Why, at the worst
Let but the queens change places ; for the one,
Three crowns and all the people at her feet
(If she act wisely) ; whilst Elizabeth
Languish in lone captivity.   The Tower,
If God so wills it.   Nay, the very block
Hath pillow'd many heads of our true faith
Whilst we walk'd young and lusty !   E'en the block,
If Heaven so wills, not the assassin's knife.

BALLARD *(ironically)*.

Were it not better at once to withdraw your name
and countenance from so dangerous an enterprise ?
Let us first think of our own heads, and when they
are sure 'twill be time enow to work for the kingdom

of Christ. Oh England, England ! How art thou
changed, and thy one-time flower of chivalry, since
thou groanest under a heretic prince !

TITCHBORNE.

Sir, I have no words for one who calls me coward
from under a priest's habit. I cannot strike, so I
am dumb. Farewell, my friends, I have to journey
to-morrow into South Hants, and I must be a-bed
betimes.

BABINGTON (*producing pencil and paper*).

First, I must have the turn of your head, the
cut of your beard, and the tip of your pearl earring
[*sketching hastily*]. Thus—my picture is well-nigh
completed, and our queen will now have a sure
way of knowing our faces. She need no longer
think of us as a pack of featureless churls. See,
a goodly company ! Will her grace recognise
amongst them the smooth-faced boy who was her
page at Sheffield grown to man's estate ? Folks say
I am but little changed, save in my stature.

[*Passing the sketch to* TITCHBORNE.

TITCHBORNE.

A pretty fancy. I recognise you as our head

in the centre. But have you any safe way of conveying this to her Majesty?

BABINGTON.

A way most sure and safe. Heaven is certainly with us. [*Drawing.*

TITCHBORNE.

Should these hurried lines not suffice for thee, we might complete the work in Hampshire, whither, as I have said, I go to-morrow, and where I should be proud to be host to you, Anthony. There are many things on which I would converse at mine ease.

BABINGTON.

The picture must be despatched at once, whilst this sure method is open to us; but if you will not journey too early in the day, I shall most gratefully avail myself of your hospitality. I myself am bound, ere long, to journey towards your Hampshire.

TITCHBORNE.

Then we journey together. To-morrow we will communicate. Once more, good evening, gentle-men. [*Exit.*

BABINGTON (*to* BALLARD).

Nay, he is as brave as our bravest. It is not for his own neck he fears; he hath a wife and child.

BALLARD.

Whom you did wrong, Babington, to recall at such a moment to his mind. The woman hath doubtless been working upon him. Oh, I know these women-folk! They have blasted the soul of many an honest man. But let us turn from the ominous gruntings of this Hampshire hog—let him wallow in his Southampton mire.

BABINGTON.

As gallant a gentleman as ever stepped.

BALLARD.

Marriage may have marred him; and yet Brutus was no bachelor! But now to what is nearest our hearts.

BABINGTON.

That is our queen's letter. It hath been nearest to mine for the week. See! its edges fray already and threaten my lady's sweet words.

[*Kisses the letter.*

BALLARD.

When to the love of woman is join'd the love
of God, the true faith, and the good of all Christendom, love on. But ere we band together in this
greatest cause, each of you is bound, I hold, to
forswear the love of all such sweethearts and courtesans as mar the dreams of young men. You should
all swear this on God's word. Oh ! I have known
women—— but I would have you to know that
it is possible for our divine love towards the blessed
Mother of God so to incorporate itself and become
incarnate, even in the fleshly nature of man, to the
utter casting out of baser desires.

BABINGTON (*thoughtfully*).

Even so—even so—I begin to credit your words.
My soul seems at length attuning itself to this grand
mystery, and, my earthly queen acting as mediator,
I doubt not I may hope to climb from her love to
that of her blessed namesake the queen of heaven.

BALLARD.

That is as it should be. So a young man fix
his eyes on heaven, I blame him not if he remember
some of the stars were women. But let us now

drink to the extinction of such lesser lights as must lead to damnation. Here's to the steeling of our hearts 'gainst all those that were wont to soften them ! We want our hearts, gentlemen.   [*Drinks.*

CONSPIRATORS.

Aye, and our heads !

[*All drink, passing the flagon.* BABINGTON *hesitates.*

Voice of ALICE (*heard without*).

I have word of a gentleman being here, with whom I would speak. Can you show me to his presence, good sir ?

LANDLORD.

How, think you, fair mistress, should I know your gentleman from the fourscore or so that frequent us nightly ? How may I know your gentleman ?

ALICE.

He is a young gentleman of noble carriage, I have heard say there is not one like him—no, not in all England.

LANDLORD.

Ah ! I'll be bound a very paragon of beauty !

You must make a pretty couple. But how tall is
your gentleman?

ALICE.

He would stoop at your door, yonder, through
which I have been privily informed he passed an
hour ago. May I speak with him?

LANDLORD.

There was [an old man, gray-bearded and cloak'd,
who stooped at my door. I noted him as straight
and tall for his years, though he walk'd with a stick.

ALICE (*suspecting*).

Ah! that is, belike, his father. Is he within there?

LANDLORD.

He is carousing with some dozen of his boon
companions; were I a young gentlewoman, I would
keep clear of them.

ALICE.

His gray hairs will protect me. May I enter?

[*Knocks.*

BALLARD.

Who knocks?

ALICE.

I would speak with one of you gentlemen.

C

BABINGTON (*aside*).

Alice !

BALLARD (*unlocking door*).

Your gentleman is not amongst us, my good girl,
but satisfy yourself.

ALICE (*after scanning each face attentively*).

To any of you doth the name of " Alice,"
Of one sweet moonlight night, of an old house
In Dorsetshire, amidst its flat park lands—
Crow-crested elm-trees clust'ring round its wings—
Of a dim chamber wainscoted with books,
Of an old woman reading from God's word
With Luther's mind, as sanction'd by King Harry,
Of a young maiden kneeling at her feet,
And list'ning to her words : to none of you
Twelve present gentlemen, do all these things
Seem to mean anything ?

CONSPIRATORS.

To none of us !

ALICE.

Alas ! to none of you ?   Then can my heart
Have so deceiv'd me ?   [*Aside*] Nay, he must be here !

Think, gentlemen, again, I pray of you—
The name of Alice?

BALLARD.

Hark you, Alice, then—
So that you rest as pure as when you came,
Take yourself hence, this is no place for you.
These gentlemen are somewhat gone in wine.
So that they deem you not some fly-by-night,
Go, get you hence!   [*Rises.*

ALICE.

Sir, all these gentlemen
Seem sober as yourself. I fear them not,
Knowing he is amongst them.

BALLARD (*angrily*).
Out, girl, out!

ALICE.

Yet if he knows not me, maybe he knows
This ring—his coat of arms. Not long ago——

BALLARD.

This passes patience! Here, mine host! Since
when hath your house so lost its good name, that

C 2

barefaced courtesans may come and molest honest
gentlemen as they sup? Out with this brazen
wench !

> [*Endeavours to thrust* ALICE *towards
> the door.* BABINGTON *rises up to
> defend her, and in so doing, his
> disguise falls from him.*

ALICE (*recognising him*).
Anthony !

> [*Clings to him for protection, whilst*
> BABINGTON *makes a gesture to keep
> off the rest.*

SCENE II.—*An anteroom at Court.* Two Courtiers
in conversation. Evening.

1ST GENTLEMAN.
Good ev'ning, sir ; you do not wear a mask ?

2ND GENTLEMAN.
I only wait to speak with Mr. Walsingham.
I am not of the company to-night.

1ST GENTLEMAN.

Then let us wait here, in this anteroom,
Whence he and all the other notables
Must pass towards the presence.

2ND GENTLEMAN.

He will pass,
Knowing I wait him.   He confides to me,
To-night, a letter to Lord Shrewsbury,
Touching the Queen of Scots.   I start to-morrow
Upon an embassage to Tutbury,
Bearing his papers.

1ST GENTLEMAN.

What think you of Shrewsbury?

2ND GENTLEMAN.

True as tried steel—all Papist tho' he be.
He is too near this queen to see in her
Aught save the painted Jezebel she is.
He sickens of her whims—as well he may—
Seeing a woman one day make her bath
Of good veal broth amidst the starving poor,
And then of wine.   Why, waste is not the word!
And all to smooth her wrinkles, so they say,

And thus inflame the hearts of foolish boys,
Who die for her ere they have seen the face
She smooths for them !

1ST GENTLEMAN.

Nor will they ever see it.
Nor her head crown'd as they would have it crown'd ;
She smooths it for the headsman.   Mark my words !

2ND GENTLEMAN.

Well, so she must coquette, no matter how ;
It may as well be with the headsman's axe,
For that will kiss her close for good and all.

1ST GENTLEMAN.

Hush ! she *may* still reign over us.

2ND GENTLEMAN.

Ah well,
If so (we live in times of change, good sooth !)
I'll never see her wrinkles, and if needs,
I'll kiss her all as closely as the axe.
We live in times of change.   [*Whistles.*

1ST GENTLEMAN.

Yet God is merciful—most merciful !
This is for some good end.   'Tis often thus.

I, in mine own short life, an hundred times
Have seen how Satan's Babel Tow'r of cards
Fell as he rais'd the topmost card.

2ND GENTLEMAN.

A queen ?

1ST GENTLEMAN.

Ha, ha !   A queen or knave, or sometimes both.

2ND GENTLEMAN.

God raises kings; these queens are of the devil—
They have such whims and such infirmities.

1ST GENTLEMAN.

Hush, hush ! thou knowest they are none the less
The Lord's anointed.   All things have a purpose ;
And e'en a scourge may guide us the right way.

2ND GENTLEMAN.

I am awearied of these wholesome scourges.
If the Lord's mercy would but grant we went
Right of ourselves !   I hold with none of this.

1ST GENTLEMAN.

I hold with it just now for my head's sake.
Once off, this head of mine will gabble treason
And blasphemies enow, I warrant you.

I feel my lips will not keep ever silent ;
But till the day that I am cleft asunder
I am a Protestant and queen's good courtier.

2ND GENTLEMAN.

Methought anon you were for all these things,
Being foreshadow'd in the Word of God ?

1ST GENTLEMAN.

Another time I will expound to you
The contradictions that there seem in me.
Not now, not now ; these very walls have ears,
And might betray my idle words.   But hush !
Here comes the topmost card in Satan's pack.

[*Enter the* EARL OF LEICESTER, *dressed in magnificent
costume.*]

2ND GENTLEMAN.

Good night, my lord.   It were vain to ask how
the world fares with one of so pleasant a countenance.

LEICESTER.

Thanks, my good friend.   I am as well as a man
may be in troublous times—his brain so harassed by
the State's complexion that he hath no time to mark

that of his own face. Happy that only a few thus sweat for the million.

1ST GENTLEMAN.

My lord is the very Atlas of our State. This is well known—the masses speak of it.

LEICESTER.

Nay, then, they are not so dunder-headed as I deemed. Her Grace is at the helm. I watch the stars.

1ST GENTLEMAN (*aside*).

Were I a fiery star whose writhing tail must switch the earth, he would not watch me long for lack of eyes.

2ND GENTLEMAN (*aside*).

Report saith he knows as little of the real state of the realm as may be with one so pampered, and that her grace will show him rather the colour of her garters than that of her mind.

LEICESTER.

Good ev'ning, sirs. I pass into the presence.

1ST AND 2ND GENTLEMEN.

Your servants, good my lord.

[*Exit* LEICESTER.

[*Enter* SIR F. WALSINGHAM.]

WALSINGHAM (*giving paper to* 2ND GENTLEMAN).

Here is the letter
Of which I spoke ; give it my lord of Shrewsbury,
With loving greeting.   Rest not by the road,
And bring his answer to me presently.
Saddle to-morrow early, and be sure
You take the safest way.

2ND GENTLEMAN.

Your servant, sir ;
I do as you desire me, and depart
To make me ready.

[*Exeunt the two* GENTLEMEN.

[*Enter* CECIL.]

CECIL.

Ah ! good ev'ning, Walsingham !

WALSINGHAM.

Hast heard these papist cries of exultation
That echo thro' the land ?

CECIL.

To me the cries
Of tinkling cymbal.   Mark me, blatant brass.

WALSINGHAM.

Hast heard their threats directed 'gainst the life
Of the queen's highness ?

CECIL.

Measured to a cry !
Mark me, cried only to excite the masses
To some untoward act, reactionary
Against the Catholics ; who henceforth, wrong'd
(As they will prove), will wear a martyr's mien
And spur their partisans to contumacy.
Such seem to me to mean these late reports
Floating around us—idle, aimless threats,
Made for a purpose.

WALSINGHAM.

Yet it might be well
To fence her highness, were it but to prove
My thought the more unmeaning ; for to *me*
These seem less idle threats than warning words,
Flung e'en to warn Her Highness.   Making sure

To spill her blood, it even seems to me
Their hearts wax pitiful, and counting her
E'en as the hang'd who walks to meet his death,
They make a truce of hatred, for the queen
Feeling that full forgiveness men may feel
Towards one doomed to die, e'en if in life
He crossed their purpose.

CECIL.

I am with you there,
To fence Her Highness from all shadow of harm.
But she is hard to fence.   Such iron courage
Mix'd often with such flippancy of mood,
I marvel at the medley.

WALSINGHAM.

Ah, forsooth
Her Highness is a woman.

CECIL.

Aye, indeed,
The very veriest woman in the land !

[*Exit* CECIL.

WALSINGHAM (*musing*).
I had a mind to tell him of my plot

To counterplot these plotters.   Yet maybe
'Tis yet o'er soon, each moment makes more ripe.
Yet, as I wait, the queen's most precious life
May be in jeopardy.   See, here they stand.
          [*Opens paper with the picture by* BABINGTON.
Curse you for traitors !   Yes, I see his face
Whom but an hour from now I saw abide
A bow-shot from her !   Who may say the names
Of those whose faces start not, like his own,
To my remembrance ?   Ah, he comes this way.
Now to dissemble !

          [*Enter* ROBERT BARNWELL.]

                    BARNWELL.
                    Ah, good ev'ning, sir !
A splendid entertainment, well conceived.
In my poor country such high junketing,
With so great hospitality, withal
So merrily attuned, had bred, with time,
A spirit far more loyal than exists
In that misguided land towards the queen.
Such bravery makes Irish loyalty.

WALSINGHAM.

Is Irish loyalty in aught allied
To loyalty in England?

BARNWELL.

It is said
An Irish heart, newly awakening
To loyalty, love, honour, duty, hate,
Or vengeance, stays at nothing.

WALSINGHAM.

So, indeed!
But they avenge, at times, e'en benefits
With thrust of knife or blow of knotted club
In that your Ireland.

BARNWELL (*lightly*).

There be caitiffs, sir,
And knaves—born knaves—in all lands o' the earth.
They lurk in court and camp, and not alone
'Midst my gray mist-capp'd mountains—this is truth.
Your servant, sir, good ev'ning!

WALSINGHAM (*aside*).

Ah, too true!
" They lurk in court and camp—and this is truth."
[*Aloud*] Your servant, sir, good ev'ning! [*Aside*] Ah,
    I would

I could unmask the traitor !   Yet at present
My one thought is to let her highness know
Her near destruction, meditated e'en
By those she fear'd the least.   I hear the strains
Of merry-making music.   Now to show
My fears less idle than she deem'd.   God grant
I find her highness predisposed to list
To my entreaties.   [*Exit* WALSINGHAM.

[*Enter* EDWARD WINDSOR.]

BARNWELL.

Well, my brother-in-arms !

WINDSOR.

How goes the cause ?   No need to say to *you*
Our watchword of green Yule and harvest time,
And yet, God speed the harvest !

BARNWELL.

So say I.
And yet there doth appear to hang some charm
About her life.   I was as near to her
To-day as now you stand—the wherewithal
To do the deed I held tight in my grasp—

When, lo ! I met her eye ; it made me quail.
She is King Harry's daughter.

WINDSOR.

Some do say
She was but father'd on him.

BARNWELL.

Nay, I knew
One who, in liquor, used to say he knew
The late King Henry, and I feel assured
This queen proceeds from him.   A royal temper—
A real right royal temper.

WINDSOR.

You, indeed,
Seem not to breathe in vain the air of courts—
You know to flatter even while you stab.

BARNWELL.

Yes, we have flattered her grace.   We have fawned
upon her, and come near to stabbing her with a
knife ; we have called her a lily and a rose ; her two
buck teeth have been call'd pearls, and her hair
gold.

WINDSOR.

I have christened her a very queen of quicksilver—
there is none can change like the queen.   But stay
—by the sound of the music methinks she hath
enter'd the ball-room.   I wish you well, and success
to your undertaking.   *[Exeunt.*

SCENE III.—*A Ball-room at Court—masks, mummers,
musicians, &c.*   CECIL, WALSINGHAM, LEICESTER.
QUEEN ELIZABETH *on the arm of* SIR CHRISTOPHER
HATTON.

ELIZABETH (*perceiving* WALSINGHAM *and* CECIL, *who
wish to obtain a hearing*).

Well, Mr. Timidity, what now?   You and Mr.
Propriety have been dogging our footsteps for the
night.   One of you hath had, doubtless, in view
care of my life, t' other of my honour.   Oh, I know;
I will not be gainsaid.   So far so good.   It hath
been said of us, however, that we have the mind of
a man, though housed in these poor rags of woman-
hood.   Of some who live in trunk-hose we have
heard said they had the souls of women.   We will

D

not say that you two gentlemen are thus chicken-
livered. First we will answer those who would
have care for our life. Are we, or are we not, the
daughter of King Harry?

CECIL (*bluntly*).

Your majesty has always been accounted his
daughter, and of late years his daughter born in
wedlock.

ELIZABETH.

Answered as though *cum grano salis.* Well, then,
we have been accounted the daughter of King Harry
by those who by their language would fain we had
been another's, so it were not their own. *Ergo,* we
are the daughter of King Henry. What say you,
my lord of Leicester? Nay, by that cuff on his
addled pate he knows us for the daughter of King
Harry! [*Cuffs him*].

LEICESTER.

Your majesty is the daughter of King Harry.

ELIZABETH (*continuing*).

Then do I fear for my life, gentlemen? I shall
answer, Did my royal father fear harm of any

amongst those that wished him ill? Did he fear
the Pope, or Antichrist, or all the combined powers
of Europe? Neither do I fear them. Let them do
their worst. Vex not yourselves for me—nay, 'tis
maybe but of small account.   [*Weeps.*

SIR C. HATTON.

Nay, madam.   [*Kissing her hand.*

ELIZABETH (*sharply*).

Nay, sir; we are King Harry's daughter.

[*Boxes his ears.*

SIR C. HATTON (*holding his hand to his head*).

Her grace hath strange moods—a very woman,
a very woman!

ELIZABETH.

S'death, man! What do we hear you muttering
below breath? " A very woman! a very woman!"
Out, man! We are no woman! It hath been said
of us that we had the mind of a man.

LEICESTER.

Her highness's varying moods recall alternately
the smiles of Venus and the thunders of Jove.

ELIZABETH (*smiling*).

Strange ! that hath been said of us before. But now for the second clause of our argument. As regardeth our honour, are we, or are we not a virgin queen ?

WALSINGHAM.

Your grace having presently signified that you were not a woman, it is difficult so to reconcile your declarations as to give satisfaction to your highness ; thus I can but make answer that your highness hath ever been accounted a virgin.

ELIZABETH.

Zounds ! Answered again as with a grain of salt. Since when such contumacy ?

SIR C. HATTON.

Your majesty is the daughter of King Harry, and a man and a virgin.

WALSINGHAM (*aside*).

Cum grano salis.

ELIZABETH.

Then what fears have ye, mine honest well-wishers, for for my life or honour ?

WALSINGHAM.

Dear madam, could I ask a moment's truce to
this light mood. I have that to speak about to
sadden your highness. I grieve to trespass on time
meant for merrymaking, but I am left no choice.
Might I have audience of your highness alone?

ELIZABETH.

We will pass towards the anteroom. But, good
Walsingham, be not long-winded. [*They proceed towards the corner of the apartment.* Nay, before you
speak I know what you would say—another Popish
plot? Nay? What then? [*Snatching at the paper
with the picture by Babington.*] Ha! who are these
pretty young gentlemen? One, two, three, four, five,
six—twelve of them.

WALSINGHAM (*sadly*).

Madam, such levity doth ill beseem
One seated so above us, on a throne
Still insecure and threaten'd. Let the child
Trample the daisy-wreath he calls a crown,
Or split the sceptre that was once a reed.
Your highness plays with nations' destinies,
And should consider. Precious is the life

Of a high princess to her faithful few ;
But precious, too, that life to Protestants
Who war with Antichrist, and to the realm—
An orphan, madam, dry-nursed with rough hands,
Should you abandon it.   I have said my say.
Think of the Prince of Orange.   In a word,
Madam, those dog your steps who seek your life.
Deign but to cast your gracious eyes hereon.

[*Presents the* QUEEN *with a paper.*

ELIZABETH.

Another letter from the Queen of Scots !
See how her spider's web of sly-fox French
Creeps o'er the paper !   And to whom this letter ?

WALSINGHAM.

Deign but to glance at present to the end,
And certify its signature.

ELIZABETH.

We mark
Her well-known signature—the " Mary R.,
Queen Dowager of France."

WALSINGHAM.

And maybe queen
Of *England* also, if we find no means

To circumvent her.   Madam, let the pray'rs
Of those who have at heart, besides their love
And loyalty towards you, love of God,
Of England, of its old-establish'd laws—
Let these prevail, and urge your majesty
To prudent measures, and to just restraint,
Directed where we need it most.   Behold
These twelve young gentlemen.

ELIZABETH.
And are these too—
These pretty gentlemen, well dress'd and shaven—
Our hidden enemies?   Ah, there is he,
The Irishman who fix'd us with his stare
To-day at Richmond [*recognising* BARNWELL'S *portrait.*]

WALSINGHAM.
All these gentlemen
Are sworn together, madam, to complete
The work begun in Holland.   They are sworn,
Under the guidance of the Scottish queen,
To work your ruin.   Even where we stand
Stood one, a moment hence, who held conceal'd
The dagger that should make her claim secure.

ELIZABETH.

She cannot be so base, good Walsingham ;
Nor will we for one moment do such wrong
To her intelligence.   *She* seek our life
Whom we (maybe from no great sister-love,
But rather awe of that estate of queen,
The which we also share) protected twice,
First, from her angry Scots, who, as a hare
Is mangled by the fierce besetting hounds
Save for the huntsman, so had mangled her,
And torn her limb from limb ; she had lain cold
Amongst her kingly kindred, but for us.
And then, against her own delinquencies—
Her murders, falsehoods, foul adulteries—
Which had leaped forth to scare the waiting world
From proofs these hands kept closed.   The Queen of
        Scots !
She seek our life !   What ! murder her first friend ?
Nay, nay ! we will not credit it !

WALSINGHAM.
                Alas !
I fear me, madam, 'tis a sorry truth ;
But time will test it.

ELIZABETH.

She will stand the test.
Zounds, sir ! we who are woman understand
A woman's dire temptations—husbanded
Thrice by the priest, and often by the will
Of wanton fancy.   There be tangled webs
Woven of wantonness, good Walsingham ;
And we can credit that there should at times
Arise the wish to sever such as these.
Yet, were we not her one defending voice ?
And would she silence it ?   What ! add our blood
To that with which her hands are reeking red ?
We cannot deem her fool as well as false.
Let all the strength of her intelligence
Protest against it !   Let the wailing voice
Of all the victims slain for love of her
Protest against it !   Let those murder'd men
Protest against it !   Murray, her own brother !
Nay, let the strangled wraith of Henry Stewart
Arise from out the ashes of his doom,
And blaze the bloody work of Kirk o' Field
To the four quarters of the winds of heaven,
To damn her that was merciless, and so
Protest against it !

WALSINGHAM.

Madam, every voice
Must needs protest against it, 'mongst the just
In heav'n and earth ; it rests but with your grace
To see that they do not protest too late.

ELIZABETH.

What is your plan of action ?   Would to heav'n
We could dispense with hurdle, gallows, block,
And quart'ring knife !

WALSINGHAM.

The times are young for that,
I fear, your grace.   Tho' should you ask me when
England may hope foreshadowing of peace,
With shooting ear of plenty in her sheaves,
I could but thus make answer, 'gainst my wish—
When God shall will that Mary Stuart shall die,
Or your great wisdom haste the certain doom
Of all humanity.

ELIZABETH.

Nay, you and Cecil
Seem but to see in queens mere common folk.

WALSINGHAM.

We sometimes see in them, your majesty,
Folk over-lenient, foolishly o'er-fond,
And over-trustful; whilst in some we see
Folk turbulent, assuming, serpent-tooth'd,
Malignant, fawning, murderous, and false.

ELIZABETH.

Hush, hush! She is our cousin, and a queen,
And all is yet unprov'd.

WALSINGHAM.

                    Her cyphers, madam,
Are in our hands—thus may we test this queen.
Her letters, also, are conveyed to us
Ere ever they do reach their destined end.
The heinous youths portrayed upon this scroll,
We have their names, their comings and their goings
Are well beknown to us; our agents note
Their secret doings; some of them are here—
" They lurk in court and camp " (I quote the words
Of one who wist not all I knew of him).
The servant of the most determined traitor
Is in our pay, and writes us word of all.
One word, and all these vile conspirators

Are gibbeted, like noisome stoats that stink
From wayside hedges in the country lanes.
Your majesty has glanced upon the letter
Addressed to him that is the ringleader,
One Babington by name, a gentleman
Of good repute till now, in Derbyshire?
Mark well her words of comfort to his cause,
The hint as of some mystery, and then
Her gracious leavetaking, as tho' to one
Her subject and deliverer.

ELIZABETH.

Alas!

And that is he that standeth in the midst,
High-featured; he that wears the shortest hair,
The sharpest beard?

WALSINGHAM.

That one is Babington.

Upon his right is Ballard, in disguise
A seminary priest; there, at his side,
Stand Chidiock Titchborne, Windsor, Salisbury,
And many more.   Each instant that these live,
A danger to your Majesty as great
As is the biding in polluted air:

For I, who know so much, am ignorant
Of this one thing—I know not when they strike !

ELIZABETH.

Then we will be as patient as themselves,
And scorn to strike too soon.   Let them live on,
So that their plot may thicken, and involve
All those that wish our ruin.   We are bold,
And fear nor man nor devil.   Hang a warrant
Over their foolish heads, and set your trap
To test the Queen of Scotland.   Mark my words,
She will be still too wise to turn our foe.
Or if she plays us false, let her beware !
We are King Harry's daughter !   [*Exit.*

WALSINGHAM (*musing*).
                                   Aye, once more
" King Harry's daughter !"   Yet not his alone,
Child of a mother destin'd to endure
Disgrace and violence !   Was her doom ordain'd
Ere ever Henry Norris had her glove,
And weigh'd her conduct nothing in the scale
Of fate's mysterious balance ?   Who may say ?
And whether this, her daughter, wax o'er bold,
Or turn to prudent measures ?   Is all plann'd

And so decided for us, that our care
Is only wasteful worrying ?   Alas !
We see but dimly.   Yet my utmost sight
Is strain'd for England's weal, and ev'ry speck
(E'en tho' no bigger than that little cloud
Seen by the Prophet) on the furthest edge
Of England's dark horizon, must command
My keen solicitude ; and this hath grown,
E'en as a storm that flings athwart blue heav'n
The black of nether hell.   To save the queen,
With all her king-craft and her woman-whims,
Is one with saving England.   At this point
England hath need of her that is the queen.
And we have need of her—our sovereign lady.
Her faithful few, who having grasp'd their nettle,
Feel not what stings the craven-finger'd fool.
I, Walsingham, have need of her, my queen,
Who needs me also, and our English land
Hath need of Walsingham.   He will not fail !

                                            [*Exit.*

ACT II.

SCENE I.—*A library in an old country house.* ALICE
and her grandmother, MRS. BELLAMY.

MRS. BELLAMY.

But now that you are back, Alice, the sunshine
is warm again. Tell me, child, what saw you in
London ? Ah, how well I mind me ! years, years
ago ! gentlemen wore their shoes slashed then, as
King Henry was gouty. A fine man, Alice ; nay, a
fine *young* man, though when I say this you will
smile, seeing that to you he is ancient history !
How do men cut their coats now—after France ?

ALICE (*wearily*).

I know not, dearest 'mother, but methinks France
and Spain are the fashion with the Papists.

MRS. BELLAMY.

Ah well, 'tis true these be but small things, as compared to the kingdom of God! Your beauty, child, is a shadow : heed it not, as once I heeded mine. Ah ! had you gone to Court, you might have heard sad tales of me ! Well, well, one is not o'er wise at seventeen. Your grandfather was one of the handsomest men of his time. Folks praised us both.

ALICE.

And he loved you ?—above Court favour, above plots and counterplots, and brake not his faith unto you ?

MRS. BELLAMY.

Loved me ! Ah, could you but have seen his love, 'twas the talk of the town ! And then his jealousy !

ALICE.

You never gave him cause ?

MRS. BELLAMY.

Not wittingly, child, not wittingly ; but I had only to speak a kind word to a Court gallant, only to show the tip of my shoe—so (my feet were always small) only to lift my hand—so (Holbein has painted my, hand), and your grandfather seemed in one moment transformed into the Evil One. How he stormed and raved ! How he reviled and cursed me ! But I am foolish, Alice, thus to dwell on the pleasures of youth ! Read to me from the Scriptures. We wait for God's kingdom.   [*Crosses herself.*

ALICE (*reproachfully*).

Dear 'mother, remember you are now of the new faith, and these popish signs should be as nothing to you.

MRS. BELLAMY.

As you say, child, with us these things are as nothing, and I am grieved at the contumacy of your uncle, my youngest son, who will not conform himself to the Protestant faith. Howbeit, 'tis an old habit, which comes natural to one born, as I was, a Papist, and who waited, as I have told you, upon the mother of the late Queen Mary, Mrs. Bullen being my fellow-tirewoman. But tell me more of London. What did you on the eve of my wedding-day ? A day you had good cause to remember, sweet one, since without it you had not been here at my knee.

E

ALICE.

Ah, grandmother, I had a dream, and such a dream ! I shudder as I think of it ! My very flesh creeps—and it was on your wedding-day too. Do you believe, dear grandmother, in visions?

MRS. BELLAMY.

There be visions and visions, grandchild; and though nine out of ten may come of an ill-baked pasty, or of wine too young in the wood, yet we read of visions in God's word; and I have heard say that without baking or boiling, or drinking wine, there have been visions. Some are of God.

ALICE.

This was my horrid dream : I was in London—
In London and alone—and Anthony
(*My* Anthony I deem'd not long ago,
Ere he had broken faith to me and mine)
Had said to me, " Sweet Alice, I am thine
In life and death." Methought he said the words
At some high altar, but the priest was hid,
So saw I not his vestments, neither knew
If he were of the new faith or the old,
Nor wist I how the nuptial church was deck'd—
If trick'd in popish-wise——

MRS. BELLAMY.

It bodes ill luck
To dream of being in a church in white.
Go on.

ALICE.

You know 'tis good to be belov'd,
And know your true love beautiful.   Anon
You made your boast of him you wedded once—
My grandfather—his love, his jealousy,
His noble presence.   All the pride of heart
You felt in those far days before my birth
Felt I, dear mother, seeing Anthony
Stand by me, straight and tall, beside the steps
Of that high altar; but, as all my heart
Uplifted in its gratitude to heaven,
Most suddenly the altar was transform'd
Into a grilling furnace, through whose bars
The red-hot fierceness scorch'd my very cheek.
I turn'd away to shun the angry glare,
And met the fix'd eyes of the hooded priest,
Till then conceal'd—the man that married us.

MRS. BELLAMY.

It bodes a very burning up of love
To dream that you are married near a fire.

E 2

ALICE.

Hear on, sweet 'mother, so your dear gray hair
Wax not the whiter as I tell my tale.

MRS. BELLAMY.

Oh, child, a dream—only an idle dream.
We all of us have had our foolish dreams.
Mine were as strange as any.   I remember——

ALICE.

Nay, hear me out.   The hidden hooded priest
Here turn'd on me his eyes—two coals of fire—
And then I saw his face—a peelèd skull—
As though 'twere Death's own semblance—and his
      hands
Rattled against the glowing altar-rails,
Naked and fleshless, as he leant thereon,
The better to behold me.   Then the church,
Aisle, nave, and choir, seemed crowded with dim
      forms,
Shrouded and hooded, swarming thick as rooks
Gleaning a field of barley.   At the first
I thought that suddenly the sheeted dead
Had risen thousand strong from where they'd lain

Down in the damp church vaults, their tablet stones
Uplifting, for some strange accomplishment
Of God's high purpose—but, in truth, I wrong'd
The sainted dead.

MRS. BELLAMY.

What were they ?   Tell me, child.

ALICE.

Fiends, 'mother.   Could they have been else than
        fiends ?
Although their features, hidden under cowls,
Show'd not to shock me, yet methought their
        shrouds
Hung down fan-folded, like a bat's limp wing
That tires of flitting.   But e'en as I gazed
Leap'd they the fenced partitions of the aisle,
And came towards us, as a thunder cloud
Darkens the last faint patch of summer sky.
Then, sparing me, they closed on Anthony,
And drawing from beneath their folded cloaks
Falchions and pointed weapons, with the same,
With one accord, those nearest of the fiends
Cleft him asunder, as they cleave a traitor

Quick after hanging, till his sever'd head
Came rolling to me (oh, my love ! my love !),
I watching, dumb with horror, all my brow
Beading with anguish, for so warm the blood
That ran from him so lately warm with life
And love of me, I could not choose but deem
He knew and lov'd me still, and that pale brow
Held soul and sense of Anthony. My grief
Outweighing maiden fear, I stooped to kiss
And bid farewell unto my true love's face,
Deeming his dear lips waited for my kiss
And last farewell, but as I bent me down
The blackest of the demons bent him too,
And, snatching at the helpless waiting mouth
By its poor boyish undergrowth of beard,
He flung it in the furnace 'fore mine eyes,
That stared in agony.

MRS. BELLAMY.

Oh, horrible !

ALICE.

And, dearest 'mother, I, who dare not look
Even at the maim'd body of a toad
Crush'd by a cart-wheel, looking, saw all this ;

The tenderness I felt for ev'ry shred
That once had seem'd my lover, making fear
My second care—my first that he should heed,
All mangled as he was, my last fond words,
And bless me ere he burnt.   So lately lived
My Anthony, that all my mind refused
To know him kill'd ; I deem'd but his young life
Dispersed, yet sentient.   My Anthony—
Nay, twenty Anthonys, dash'd on the ground,
As one might spill red sacramental wine
(Wherein, as Papists deem, God's spirit lives,
Who worship Him in ev'ry crimson stain),
So seem'd these bleeding fragments of poor flesh
My Anthony—all marr'd and murder'd thus—
Helpless to clasp and kiss, or say farewell,
But still my Anthony—still loving me—
Not turn'd into a foe.

MRS. BELLAMY.

Most terrible !

And was he dead, his young life shiver'd thus
To twenty atoms?   Rather had it seem'd
To me, as 'twere the sacramental cup,
Dash'd by some angry demon to the ground,
Spilling God's spirit.

ALICE.

Aye, far rather this
Than that which is to follow !   Bear with me,
This memory unnerves me.

MRS. BELLAMY.

My poor child,
I marvel not that fear possess thy heart
At so great horror ; most assuredly
The Lord hath spoken to thee in a dream.

ALICE.

The worst's to come.   My only abject fear
That I might lose my love, nor let him know
Once more my love of him, I leant across
The altar rails to where the furnace glow'd,
Betwixt the iron bars whereof I saw
My Anthony's poor face, yet unconsumed,
Seeming transparent, as an agate held
This side the light ; but as I form'd my lips
Into a word of tenderness, his own
All suddenly grew to a ghastly grin,
As tho' of dire derision.   I beheld,
Glitt'ring, an angry double-row of teeth,
Saw-sharpen'd, with the furnace red behind ;

These closed on one another, as he hiss'd
The name of her he lov'd—the Queen of Scots ;
Then laugh'd a grating laugh, the which the fiends
Echoed, till all the rafters of the church
Shook with the ghastly chorus, whilst his lips
Burn'd slowly to a cinder, whose last words
Had left me doubly desolate.   'Twas then
I heard these words, deliver'd at the last,
By one whose voice rang louder than the fiends'
Harsh, shrilling laughter : " Traitor unto heav'n !
Traitor unto thy country and thy queen !
Traitor to wife and child, and fond first love !
E'en traitor unto traitors !"   And there fell
A silence, as may be the tomb's, and then
I 'woke to find myself in mine own bed,
In Fleet Street, at my cousin Willoughby's.

MRS. BELLAMY.

Indeed, indeed that were a vision sent
Of heaven as a warning !   Never dream
Boded more evil to young Anthony,
His soul and body both !   'Twere best to eschew
One so ill starr'd, my Alice !   In the days
When you two, cousin-like, must needs, forsooth,

Play carelessly at being man and wife,
Against my wishes, was there no small voice
That warn'd thee, Alice, that a youth thus fill'd
(Like to the sails of some gay privateer,
Gold-laden from the Indies, under Drake,)
With winds that blow o'er many colour'd capes
And coral-stranded isles, were no fit mate
For one whose life, like thine, has been retired
And hidden 'mongst the folk-forsaken shades
Of this old manor-house ?   Ah, 'tis a youth
Headstrong and arrogant, he stands foredoom'd.
Men say his mind is fill'd with foolishness
Since he return'd to England from abroad.
But there are other men as good as he
In England, aye, and better too, my child,
And cousins, too, upon thy father's side,
Worth ten of Anthony for steadfastness ;
Your cousin Willoughby's brave soldier-son,
Your guardian—a man of twice your years,
But none the worse for that—a steady man,
One in whose care I fain would leave my girl.
True, Anthony is rich—but what is wealth
To one attainted ?

ALICE.

Nay, that very wealth
Was what I seem'd to love in him the least.

MRS. BELLAMY.

You are a foolish child ; learn to be wise
Of one who has paid wisdom's bitter price.

ALICE.

Yet not to warn him—if indeed the voice
Of God hath spoken ! I who ne'er can be
His wife, since now another bears his name,
May I not be his guardian, to point,
If not the road to good, at least the road
That leads away from evil, maybe death ?
You would not have me husband so my breath
As that I should not waft him one good word,
But let him go his way ?

MRS. BELLAMY.

How should a maid
Pursue a young man, to unearth the thought
Deep buried in his dark ambitious soul ?
Not meeting him, it were not safe to trust
Your fears unto a letter in these days,
Since indeed (as I have heard surmised),

He herd with traitors, to admonish him
Of what might be his danger were to you
A danger likewise.   Ah ! I know these days
In which we live, who all my life have dwelt
As spied by Argus eyes !   I scarce dare *think !*
To know a traitor means to aid a traitor ;
To love a traitor means to be a traitor ;
To be a traitor means—it means the block !

ALICE (*sadly*).
The block is our most merciful escape
From these dark days.   I pray I meet no worse,
For 'tis at least an honourable death
(Since those have died on it who did no wrong),
And some say painless.

MRS. BELLAMY.
                    Those who told thee this
Had ne'er endured such painlessness.   But fie
On one of my ripe years to let you speak
Of blocks and traitors !   Out on me, I say,
For an old fool, despite my silver hair.
We scare ourselves until we almost start
At our own shadows !
                    [*Both start, hearing knock at the door.*

ALICE.

Who is it that knocks ?

[*Enter* GILES, *a servant.*]

GILES.

The dutiful compliments of Colonel Nicholas Willoughby, but lately returned from the Low Countries,
and might he visit you to-day at noon, after the
dinner hour? He is halting at the inn at the town.

MRS. BELLAMY.

At dinner, Giles ! *at* dinner ! Our cousin Willoughby ! No need, in sooth, that he should ask
ere he visit those who will be o'er ready with a
welcome ! Bid him ten thousand times welcome,
and we wait him impatiently ! [*To* ALICE.] Your
cousin Nicholas, dear child, lately returned from
the Low Countries ! He comes at a happy moment
to banish all our gloomy fears and presages !

ALICE.

I feel in no mood for him. I cannot see him.

MRS. BELLAMY.

Alice ! Your cousin Nicholas ! He who used in
the old time to call you his little wife !

ALICE.

Aye, granny, I remember it well. His "little wife," and I will never be his little wife!

MRS. BELLAMY.

A foolish child—alas! A foolish child! But girls are ever fanciful.

ALICE.

Oh grandmother! I have yet kept something back. I *did* warn Anthony; I sought him out, yea even in a common tavern-room, where he and some companions sat at wine. Old Nancy met him in Newgate Market—she would have known his voice and noble bearing amongst a thousand; yet had she doubted, Mr. Salisbury, who was with him, would have confirmed her, he being without disguise. Anthony wore not his own hair, and had a beard. She saw him enter the tavern of the "Three Tuns," whereof she apprised me, and we went there together.

MRS. BELLAMY (*reproachfully*).

Ah child, child! If I am to see you link your fate to a conspirator, I have indeed cumbered too long the earth; for I fear me report speaks but too truly, and that Anthony hath in hand some dark

dealings.   For what else his false hair and beard? or
wild Tom Salisbury his companion, whose mother
must rue the day she bore him? though, what could
be hoped from one in the following of Lord
Leicester? Ah, well-a-day ! And you, Alice, seeming
like my very own child !   [*Exeunt, sighing.*

[*After a pause, enter* COLONEL WILLOUGHBY.]

WILLOUGHBY.

Here is the dear oak room, and all unchanged
As when, a young man, all aflare with hope
Of glory in God's cause, victorious arms,
Retrievèd fortunes, and high honours won,
I join'd to these a dream of home and love,
When that fair slip of maidenhood, my ward,
Then budding into girlhood, grew to be
The woman she is now !   I marvel much
If she fulfil the promises she made
To be a beauty ?   Let me think—her age—
Her age must be by this some twenty years,—
Those seven which have snatch'd my last of youth,
And made of me this rough-hewn soldier-lout,
Have changed her to a woman.   [*Looks in mirror.*

Forty years
Mated to twenty summers ! Forty years !
And not so spent in holding dainty skeins
Of lady's silk, in chambers arras-hung,
Rustling with broider'd petticoats, that she,
This gentle child, should deign to view my suit
With eyes of favour. I shall seem to her
Only the rude campaigner that I am,
My fingers all too harsh to wind her skeins,   .
Too rough to lure sweet music from her lute,
Save at the risk of snapping all its strings
Thro' clumsy handling, and with voice too gruff
To trill a sonnet.

[*Enter* Mrs. Bellamy.

Mrs. Bellamy.

Cousin Nicholas,
Ten thousand welcomes ! Aye, and wherefore sue
Of one so proud as I to welcome you ?
Alice and I are all too pleased to bid
You, our dear cousin, to our simple board.

Willoughby.

How is my cousin Alice ?

MRS. BELLAMY.

Not o'er well. You will smile, cousin, at so much
zeal in one so young, but I do believe she is vexed
for the safety of the queen's majesty. Strange
rumours reach us from town.

WILLOUGHBY.

You are hinting at these plots to assassinate the
queen—the disaffection among the Papists. Let
my fair cousin rest; it will pass off—mere thunder
showers to herald the brighter morrow. Let them
come down, say I. [*Enter* ALICE, *unperceived.*] And
as for the traitors, we shall gibbet them, cousin; we
shall gibbet them. [*Perceiving* ALICE, *and taking her
hand.*] And so, fair cousin, we meet again. After a
rough life in rough places I find myself once more in
my boy haunts; for this old manor-house was known
to me long ere you came to gladden it. [*Aside.*] As
beautiful as one might imagine an angel !

ALICE.

And yet after all, cousin Nicholas, they have done
but little in Flanders for God's cause.

WILLOUGHBY.

All is as yet in a great uncertainty; but, as I was

F

saying to my good cousin there, these be but thunder
showers. Events will shuffle themselves right, by
God's grace. The Frenchmen vexed us somewhat—
they being but half friends, and more than half foes,
if the apple of discord may thus be split. But we
wait God's good time.

ALICE.

'Twere hazardous dealing with them, without
doubt. For me, true friend or true foe.

WILLOUGHBY.

Then, cousin, I am for you—your true friend.

ALICE.

Be not o'er rash, lest I should prove you, cousin,
in some way you wot not of. You are returning to
town ere long?

WILLOUGHBY.

Indeed I fear me, fair cousin, my stay must not
extend over to-morrow. Though we are, as it were,
disbanded, I shall not give up the soldier till these
thunder clouds clear somewhat. My services are
still at the disposal of my queen, and I am in this
part on a special mission.

MRS. BELLAMY.

Your cousin means by thunder clouds, plots, Alice
—plots which have their rise in Spain.

WILLOUGHBY.

Calm yourself, Alice. Let not these reports distress
you. A cloud of midges in the air—they bite, but
rarely draw blood. No names are as yet given (nay,
and if they were, it would ill become me to divulge
them), but from all I' hear some dozen foolish boys
are banded together in the interest of the Scottish
queen, who hath in her nature so little prudence and
reserve, as we know of old, that through indiscretion
she will betray even her own friends. But these
conspirators are but like mites in a cheese, which
may help it to seethe and fester, but which change
not its outward form. So silly women and boys can
never alter the form of the State. We want for that
the club of a giant and a master mind.

ALICE.

Alas! poor misguided young gentlemen!

WILLOUGHBY.

All we shall know of them in the after years, poor

F 2

fools, will be their quarters hoisted to scare their fellows, and their heads rotting on Tyburn Gate.

[ALICE *shudders.*

MRS. BELLAMY (*turning the subject*).

How did you travel from London? Alone?

WILLOUGHBY.

Alone, save for my body-servant, and ill-mounted (for my horse cast a shoe on Hounslow Heath, and went lame from a flint), all through the desolate country between Bagshot and Blackwater, the wind wafting to my nostrils, ever and anon, the scent of the carrion swinging on Hartford Bridge Flats, set there to frighten other malefactors, who, nevertheless, still haunt this wild tract; so was I not displeased to fall in, near Basingstoke, with two gentlemen, well mounted and armed, attended by six servants, and with them I made some of my journey, parting company at Popham Lane, where the gentlemen were met with fresh horses from Micheldever. "Take mine," said the elder of the two young gentlemen, "since I have not far to go, and have saved mine to keep your pace—so that he will easily take me a short stage further." This offer I gratefully accepted, seeing it was made with so good a grace, and by a gentleman born and bred, for then it was that I found him to be Mr. Titchborne, a Catholic gentleman of old family, living near Alton ; but as he also frequents the town, I shall hope to repay his civility.

MRS. BELLAMY.

'Tis a fine old name. I have heard say the Titchbornes have lived in South Hants and were of note before ever we were taken by the Normans.

WILLOUGHBY.

Anyhow, here was I the richer by a stout strawberry roan, Mr. Titchborne telling me he would care for my poor nag till my return ; but upon hearing my destination, says the younger gentleman, " Take heed that I do not get there before thee ! for I shall be that way myself in a day or two, and will bring you your horse, if he be cured, and take charge of my friend Titchborne's as far as Popham Lane.

MRS. BELLAMY (*to* GILES, *who enters*).

So, if a gentleman should come for Colonel Willoughby's strawberry roan, you will apprise us of

it, so that we may not be wanting in civility to him.
Young gentlemen do not come this way every day,
do they, Alice ?

ALICE.

I care not whether they come or go !   [*Exit.*

WILLOUGHBY.

And now, dear cousin, tell me of your son.   •
Had that strange rumour aught of truth in it
Wafted to me in Flanders, and which said   .
That he had gone distraught ?

MRS. BELLAMY.

He gone distraught !
A son of mine ! Why, even your whole body,
Brave tho' it be, containeth not the sense
He holds in half his hand ! Yet list to me,
I will not hide from you that he of late
Hath strangely borne him—living much apart,
With Father Harington, a Jesuit,
A learned man. And now these two together
Have often left us women to ourselves,
Too busy for the welfare of their souls
To care how their despisèd bodies fare.
He may be here anon, to eat with us,

But there are times he flies from us all day.
Yet is this godliness, not folly, cousin ;
And if at times he seems a moody man,
Silent and self-contain'd, ah, blame him not ;
For why, his thoughts are all too high for us.
His lot is hard.—And so they said distraught !—
Distraught of Jeremy, whose angry face
I would that you could look on when he knows
They said he was distraught !

WILLOUGHBY.

Nay, pardon me,
I did but ask the truth of these reports.
But what is it that makes his lot so hard ?

MRS. BELLAMY.

Well, look you, it *was* hard—he as a lad
Lov'd solitude and pray'r ; and, being born
In that old faith now crumbling, eagerly
Read he of miracles, and martyr'd men
Dying for God.   Anon this new reform
Crept o'er the land ; and, finding many of us
Waiting for purer ways of serving God,
Grew like the sweet new ripeness of a fruit
Flushing towards the light.   Yet so imbued

Was he, my second son, with his beliefs
He would have burnt for them, so kept his faith
Whilst we turn'd Protestant, seeing the day
Veil'd from his eyes.   You know he purposèd
To take the priestly vow, but then our king
Brake up the monasteries through the land.
Later ensued his elder brother's death,
Leaving us Alice only, and no son.
Then said his father, " Thou must make our house,
Nor shall I will thee aught at my decease
If thou should'st sink thy manhood in the monk ;
But baby Alice shall possess my all,
Yet even she, should she, improvident,
Wed with a Papist, shall be dispossessed.—
From this she hath been saved.

WILLOUGHBY.

How ?   Wherefore saved ?

MRS. BELLAMY.

'Tis a long tale to tell—and you had heard
Had there been aught in it of real import,
You being left her guardian.   Let it pass,
For 'tis not worth the naming.   Both were young—

Their dream is long since over—years ago—
Only a childish folly.

WILLOUGHBY.

Only that?

MRS. BELLAMY.

Aye, truly, cousin, and this in your ear—
I think, had Jeremy not been my son
Whom well I know above all base intent,
I had imagin'd that he forced her somewhat—
Threw them together—dazzled the young man.
This had I thought, had he not been my son—
Yet being son of mine, methinks his friends
Plotted thus putting Alice out of chance
Of any stray inheritance.

WILLOUGHBY.

Well, well,
But she hath truly put all this away?

MRS. BELLAMY.

I do believe it—but you know young maids
Will ofttimes nurse a shadow.   'Tis enough
For them to gaze upon a faded rose

Or kiss a tatter'd letter.   These suffice
Till some brave gentleman of flesh and blood
Scare off such phantoms.

[*Enter* ALICE.   MRS. BELLAMY *goes into another part
of the room, leaving them together.*]

ALICE.

Cousin Nicholas,
Anon you said that you were my true friend—
I ask you a friend's service.

WILLOUGHBY.

Ask not twice—
The service is perform'd.

ALICE.

It is a letter
I wish to send under your care to town.

WILLOUGHBY.

Indeed a paltry boon ! and I that hoped
You wish'd my right hand or my grizzled pate !

ALICE.

Nay, do not jest ; this is no common letter,
Nor must you tell one in the whole of England

That I entrusted it to you. 'Tis not yet writ—
I ask you first——

WILLOUGHBY.

Nay, twenty thousand letters !
I am your Mercury of the wingèd heel.

ALICE.

Nor must you let it meet a living eye,
Nor leave it carelessly to soil and fray
Here in your leathern jerkin.   Place it *there !*
[*Indicating his heart.*
It is for my near kinsman, Mr. Babington—
A private matter.   Though you know him not,
You know him, doubtless, as my mother's nephew ;
Like you, that makes him cousin ; and he lodges
Right in the way to go from Charing Cross
Over the fields to London.

WILLOUGHBY.

I obey.
Give me the letter privily and soon,
As I must start to-morrow.

MRS. BELLAMY.

They are late—
Your uncle and the Father.   Sure to-day

They will not shun our company. Good cousin,
With your permission, we will seek the terrace,
Where, should they come home by their common way,
We needs must meet them.

[*Exeunt into the garden.*

[*Enter* JEROME BELLAMY *by another door, accompanied
by* FATHER HARINGTON.]

BELLAMY.

Aha ! a few moments alone to consider ere we are
plagued with the fat heretic ! and pen and ink to
scratch a word to that die-away wench, Alice. [*Takes
up pen and writes.*] See, this will do. The most
foolish of women can hoodwink a man, so you may
trust her to lie to the trooper. [*Reads.*] " Anthony
Babington will be here in less than an hour. There
are reasons for deeming it expedient that he should
not be known as such. He hath met Willoughby
before, who yet was ignorant of his name. See that
your grandmother and the servants speak of him
as Mr. Bellingham, and thus take some trouble off
the hands of him that houses you out of charity."
Giles ! [*Calling servant. Enter* GILES.

This message to Mistress Alice. She is in the
garden. Give it her at once, and await her orders.

[*Exit* GILES *with letter.*

FATHER HARINGTON.

Mr. Babington hath a brave countenance and a
most courteous bearing.

BELLAMY.

He fatteneth on his one idea, which is to him like
good roast meat after kickshaws.

FATHER HARINGTON.

Which of the gentlemen is to kill the queen ?

BELLAMY.

There are six told off to do it, but Babington hath
the ordering of them all. Abington, Titchborne,
Barnwell, Tilney, and others. Some of them feel
anxious for the end, but it is too late to cry off
now. Tilney is for the queen being set upon in
her coach. Mr. Titchborne wishes God could be
served without killing her.

FATHER HARINGTON.

Yet he said all was progressing happily ?

BELLAMY.

So happily that the end is almost sure. The Prince
of Parma is holding himself in readiness. Our long
service has not been without plentiful fruition.

FATHER HARINGTON.

" God prosper the harvest ! "   *[Exeunt.*

SCENE II.—*A garden. Moonlight.* COLONEL
WILLOUGHBY *and* ALICE.

WILLOUGHBY.

Ah, this is such an often-fancied scene
Of perfect home contentment, that I doubt
These very eyes that look on it, and deem
The whole some fleeting vision !

ALICE.

                                  None the less
Yours is true sight, since I with mine own eyes
See this same peaceful scene, and thank God for it.

WILLOUGHBY.

Then you, sweet cousin, are content with this—
These long, white, moonlit alleys, and these bars

Of close-cropp'd cypress ?   Far beyond their shade
Know you there lies a wondrous outer world
Of toil and turmoil ?   As the nestling, warm
From her soft breast that shelter'd it from ill,
Strains o'er the edge of home and longs for wings,
Have you, dear cousin, dream'd no dream of life
Far from these flat park lands ?

ALICE.

Yes, oftentimes,
And yet, as often have I pray'd to heav'n,
To keep me from the taint of outer life.

WILLOUGHBY.

Yet outer life not always needs corrupt.
Rather, methinks, after our first hot blood,
We who have donn'd the wand'rer's sandalled shoon,
See in our sweetest dreams green waving fields,
Or some such scene as this, with one hard by
Seeming as fair as now you seem to me—
The airy shape my spirit hath adored,
Transform'd into a woman !

ALICE.

I have heard
That soldiers see in ev'ry passing form

Some such divinity. But it is late—
My grandmother has left us ; come, good cousin,
Surely my uncle has return'd by now.

          MRS. BELLAMY (*approaching*).
I dream of my young days. How fair the night !
Take care of Alice, cousin, whilst once more
I pace the ivy terrace.

            WILLOUGHBY.
          Listen, Alice,
Leave me not now, whilst my unutter'd words
Are rising nigh to choke me ! For this hour
I've seen foreshadow'd in my soldier's life,
Seeming a ray from some superior world,
Of utmost light and beauty ! Know of me
That tho' I speak the language of rude camps,
Mine ne'er hath been the knee, till now, to bend,
As you would deem, to any passing form ;
Nor have I knelt to one in woman's shape,
As now I kneel to you, sweet cousin Alice !
         [*Makes as though he would kneel.*

            ALICE.
What would you with me that you kneel to me ?
Rise, you abash me.

WILLOUGHBY:

I am all unused
To fine set-phrases ; will you be my wife ?

ALICE.

Oh ! cousin, can I be no other thing,
And so the better serve you ? since my heart
Is that one only gift I must withhold.

WILLOUGHBY.

Then, Alice, let me never see you more !
Too much has hung upon too slight a thread,
I was a fool to dream that one like you
Could stoop to love me.   Let us say farewell.

ALICE.

Ah ! cousin, are we women good for naught
Saving for wives or lovers ? and of us
Can it be never said, as of you men,
" They two are friends, they two bear right good will
One t'ward the other ? "   Must it ever be,
" They two are lovers," or, " They two are foes ? "

WILLOUGHBY.

Where is the friendship that survives the sight
Of looks forlorn, and wit that vanisheth
At one friend's coming ?

G

ALICE.

Nay, say rather this,
Where is the friendship that survives the blow
Dealt to a vanity o'er sensitive ?
For such, methinks, is your man's love of us.
And yet, too often, 'tis from no pretence
Of being better that we women shrink
From taking all you offer us ; as oft
'Tis *we* who feel unworthy so full love,
Who, maybe, have not heart to give you back.
Some may have lov'd and may not love again ;—
These are the women who are meant for friends—
True as the friend I fain would be to you.

WILLOUGHBY.

So you have also lov'd, poor child, like me ?

ALICE.

Perchance : suffice it that my heart is cold,
Nor wakes for aught save friendship ; it may be
That once, like that poor fledgling from its nest,
I, leaning o'er the moss-embroider'd stone
Of this gray terrace, flank'd with peacock yews,
Craned at the outer world, and saw my fate—
One who was born to strive beyond these bounds

Of yew and cypress.   Now all this is past ;
Nor will I say, so you should pity me,
" My heart is love-sick of a great past love,"
Since, whether love, or whether loss of love,
I know not wholly which I mourn the most ;
Yet this I know, that whilst *one* lives on earth,
And breathes, (though not for me,) his breath of life,
I ne'er will wed with other living man !

WILLOUGHBY.

Then would that he were dead !

ALICE.

                                Hush ! hush ! alas,
You know not how such evil wish may speed !
E'en now he seems to walk a man foredoom'd !

[*Enter* GILES *with a letter.   Gives it to* ALICE, *who
reads (aside) in agitation.*]

" Anthony Babington will be here in less than an
hour.   There are reasons for deeming it expedient
that he should not be known as such.   He hath
met Willoughby before, who yet was ignorant of his
name.   See that your grandmother and the servants
speak of him as Mr. Bellingham, and thus take some

trouble off the hands of him that houses you out of
charity." What strange confirming of my darkest
fears !

> [*Calls back* GILES *and explains to him*
> contents *of letter.* WILLOUGHBY
> *watching at short distance.*

To WILLOUGHBY.]
Only a homely household matter, cousin ;
We are to have another guest at supper.

WILLOUGHBY (*continuing*).
So you have lov'd, poor Alice? then for me
Feel some kind pity ; as for him you lov'd,
I ask no news of him, I want no word
To tell me who he was or what his name ;
Nay, I would rather never see his face.

GILES (*throwing open window leading into garden*).
Mr. Bellingham.

[*Enter into the garden* BABINGTON, BELLAMY, MRS.
BELLAMY, *and* FATHER HARINGTON.]

WILLOUGHBY (*aside*).
My fellow-trav'ller, who, with Chidiock Titchborne,

Rode with me through the moorlands of South
Hants !
Yet how the sudden sounding of his name
Came like the answer to my hasty words !
[Exeunt into the house, through the window.

SCENE III.—BABINGTON *standing alone at the deserted
supper-table, a broken wine-cup on the floor.*

[Enter ALICE.]

BABINGTON (*raising wine to his lips*).
Your health, cousin Alice, and a handsome hus-
band from amongst the young men you may favour !
[Drains the cup.

ALICE (*sadly*).
What is the worth of a young man's love ?

BABINGTON (*scornfully*).
Oh, we all know it hath in it none of the force
or the fire of a maiden's; and she will love in such
pretty ways too—trying for the letter of his name
with a snail crawling over a slate, or flinging over her
shoulder the peel of an apple to see in what form
it will fall !

ALICE.

It hath never fallen as an A.

BABINGTON.

No, nor a B. either with me !

ALICE.

What, did *you* ever try for my name ?

BABINGTON.

First tell me how long since you tried for mine ?

ALICE.

Why think at all of what was so long ago ?

BABINGTON.

Are we, then, now grown so wise ? Our letters are the same, Alice—A.B.—A.B. Is there no subtle meaning, think you, herein ?

ALICE.

It was meant that we should never be joined, save by the links of friendship. You have heard of the saying—

If you change your name and not your letter
You change for the worse and not for the better.

This is a saying that they have down in Kent.

BABINGTON (*passionately*).
What care I, Alice, for the men of Kent ?
What care I if the whole of England join'd,
Strong-tongued and vehement, to shriek the words,
You two are never to be link'd together ?
Should I believe, or lend an ear to that
I knew was false ?

                    ALICE.
                              Nay, listen, Anthony,
I fain would speak with you—not many words ;
I come to supplicate you on my knees
To speak of this most horrid mystery,
Which seems to suck you to its hidden depths
As would a whirlpool.   Something is amiss,
And threatens England whilst it threatens you.
Now, tho' I never can be wife of yours,
Tho' all the love that liv'd betwixt us two
Is shiver'd like yon crystal drinking-cup,
Yet in my woman's heart some echo stays
The which your footfall wakes ; some little pearl,
Toss'd by the tempest, ling'ring after storm,
To mind me that I lov'd you once—and thus
I would befriend you.   Hear these few poor words
From your true sister-cousin.   May she speak ?

BABINGTON.

Speak on—speak ever in those silv'ry tones,
So sister-calm ! And hath it come to this
Betwixt us two, who swore nor life nor death
Should ever part us ? Hath it come to this,
" Your sister-cousin ?" and am I to rest
Contented with a sermon ? Preach your best—
I listen to your words, but mark you, Alice,
I give no chilly brother-love for yours.

ALICE.

You being husband, father, and *my* cousin,
Will list to words of reason, nor renew
A foolish dream we 'woke from years ago
(Full four long years), wherefrom you 'woke the first.

BABINGTON.

"Wherefrom I 'woke the first !" And what were we
Those four years since, my Alice ? What were we ?—
A girl and boy playing with but the shadow
Of this dear night's reality.

ALICE (*reproachfully*).

Oh, cousin,
Think of your wife who loves you, and your child !

BABINGTON.

Were you this incarnation of all light,
All majesty, all beauty, all repose ?
Was I the man who now, here at your feet,
Cries to your heart for pity ?   Since those days
I have seen women who were counted fair,
Living in courts and camps and convent-walls,
And I have wander'd forth thro' many lands,
Dreaming my dreams of man's strange purpose here,
Seeking the shadow of the one ideal,
The which I clasp to-night !

[*Endeavouring to embrace her.*

ALICE.
Oh, Anthony !
For love of all your saints, leave go your hold !

BABINGTON.

Then say you do not love me, looking thus
Into these eyes that hunger, say the words——

ALICE.
I do not love you.

BABINGTON (*excitedly*).
How ! You dare to lie,
Thus looking at me ?   But your beating heart
Tells me you lie !   Thank heaven that you lie !

ALICE.

Oh, Anthony, I leave you ! You are mad—
The wine has turn'd your brain. Think of your wife.

BABINGTON.

Look you—my wife is nothing to my heart
Compared to what you are : for worthiness,
True-heartedness, and kindness are not *love*.
Love is a master-passion, and obeys
No tyrant rein nor spur ; you lov'd me, Alice—
And now my heart is ripe to meet your love.
I know the nothingness of all my aims,
And kneel to you for mercy.

[*Kneeling and clasping her hands.*

ALICE (*with emotion*).
What would you ?
Your words are as a madman's !

BABINGTON.
This would I—
My horse is ready saddled, and the night
Will curtain us, save for yon rising moon.
You are my more than life. I may not live
Without your love. Come, bless a broken life—

Be the old loving Alice of the past,
And naught shall separate us.

ALICE.

Fly with you ?—
Now!—leave my uncle's house !—leave honour, friends,
For one who cannot even be mine own !
Become an outcast—plunge in misery
A virtuous lady and her innocent babe !
Your child—your child—ah ! has he eyes like yours ?
I shall be never wife and never mother !   [*Weeps.*

BABINGTON.

This, then, was all your boasted love of me.
Oh, what a light and overrated thing
Is woman's love !—most, women that are fair !
How do they deal in phrases neatly set,
And call it loving, whilst their hearts beat cold
A measured tune beneath their bodices—
Those buckram bulwarks that so well defy
Our boldest sallies !   [*Laughs hoarsely.*

ALICE (*shuddering*).

Nay, nay! laugh not thus !
Such laugh is crueller than fifty frowns,

The while I see your angry glitt'ring teeth
Seeming saw-sharpened.

BABINGTON.

So you drive me hence,
I and this poor unwelcome love of mine.
You wish me hence ?—say it with your own lips !

ALICE.

I wish you hence ! I do not love you ! Go !

BABINGTON.

I go.   But, Alice, listen to my words—
I go to what will doubtless seem to you
A sure perdition.   Yet are you the cause,
Since you could save me.

ALICE (*eagerly*).

Save you ?   Tell me how !
I would give——

BABINGTON (*interrupting*).

Words again—mere woman's words !
You that seem'd ready once to cede your soul
Shrink now from hazarding that wav'ring thing
Gone with a breath, like spring's most fragile flower,
Or braving unabash'd the fiercest storms—

At once the fairest, falsest, foulest thing—
A woman's reputation !

ALICE.

                    Scorn me not,
But say, how may I serve you ?

BABINGTON.

                    Look you here,
I will admit I had forgot how fair
Had seem'd the face that lured me when a lad.

ALICE.

You only lov'd my *face* ?

BABINGTON.

                    Not that alone—
Soul, mind, and body, you were meant for me.
Yet had you left me wholly, it may be
I had forgotten.   But you could not rest,
Being a woman from your topmost thread
Of auburn hair down to your pretty shoe,
And so you said, " I will not let him rest,
He shall not thus get quit of me."

ALICE.

                    Indeed,
I never thought to look upon you more !

BABINGTON.

And for this reason, at the evening hour
You sought me in a tavern ; blinding me
With such a blaze of unexpected light,
You shook my best endeavours.   It was strange—
My comrades, drinking, swore for evermore
To bury all their foolish earthly loves,
And cling alone to her that reigns in heaven—
They drank, but as the wine cup pass'd to me
I heard your voice, and pausing, did not drink.

ALICE.

Would you had drank of it ! then had you now
Spared me for your vow's sake.   What ! did I sin
So deeply, loving once, that you should scorn
And curse me now ?

BABINGTON.

Alice, I curse you not,
'Tis I am cursed by you.   To you is given
The saving of me, but you scorn the task.
Now listen to me, and behold what hangs
· On your girl-wisdom !   Ah, not *I* alone
Await your will, but England, and the queen,
With half her nobles.   As you see me now,

I am that Babington of whom hereafter
It will be said, he suffer'd for the cause
Of God and true religion ; in a word,
I am the one head mover in this scheme,
Hatch'd nigh to breaking forth, to kill the queen !'

ALICE (*in horror*).
To kill the queen ! Elizabeth, the queen !

BABINGTON.
To kill the queen of England.   All is plann'd,
The train is laid, it only needs the match
(The which I hold or else withhold) to fire ;
Then for that Babington whom men will name
In grateful hist'ry's bolder after-page,
Rich guerdon and renown, and high estate,
Should heaven prosper us.   This I renounce
For love of you ; I lay it at your feet,
Deeming you richer spoil than all the gold
Of Philip's Indies—this, if all succeed ;
But if it pleaseth God to chasten us,
Humbling our hopes, because too rainbow-hued,
Then for that Babington whom the future page
Of servile hist'ry will denounce as base,
Regicide, villain, unregenerate.

The blight of early doom made terrible,
A cloven traitor's writhing agony—
This save me, Alice.

ALICE.

Oh, you torture me !
Your love of me is cruel as the rack !

BABINGTON.

See what you damsels fondly set against
Your boasted maiden-honour in the scale !
How precious is that pure virginity
You save for someone !

ALICE.

Nay, you scorn'd it once,
And shall I prize what you have flung aside ?
I have before me honour, duty—these,
And more, the honour that I owe your wife,
The love methinks I yet must bear your child.
Ask me to die for you.

BABINGTON.

To die for me !
To die for me !   That any fool could do.
Nay, live for me, and reign my queen of loves !
For you I leave all honours and renounce

All dangerous designs.   Ah, Alice, come,
Come to these arms that wait you !-

ALICE.

Anthony,
I prithee leave me, or I leave you first !

BABINGTON (*moving towards window*).
I leave you, and I leave all good with you.
I go, my soul despoilèd of its wings.
You drive me from you for you do not love me,
I go to meet my destiny.   Farewell !
                    [*Exit out of window into garden.*

ALICE.
He goes to meet his destiny !   Just heav'n,
Why dost Thou try me ?   Ah, I " do not love ! "
Not love you, Anthony ?   God help my love !
God help us both !
                    [*Falling on her knees—continuing.*
                    Aye, what is this poor form
Of fainting, hesitating flesh and blood,
That I should set it thus against the State,
Against his dearest will, who seem'd to me
Once, more than queen and England all in one ?
Nay—it is less than nothing !   Still to wrong

H

One I have never seen, yet one I know
Noble and worth his loving. But the State—
" The queen with half her nobles," is not this
Of more importance to the nation's good
Than even that pure life with all its trust ?
Ah, help me, heaven ! since my senses blurred
Refuse to lend me light !
> [*Rising from her knees.*

I have a plan
Whereby to save him ! What is this poor life,
This vaunted maiden-honour ? For his sake
I will so shame myself in all men's eyes
As that they scoff at me, e'en tho' he own
Naught that is mine save this weak, falt'ring hand,
The which I pray may guide him ! Yes, my pray'rs,
My tears shall move him. I will kneel to him,
Nor leave him till he swear by ev'ry saint
To shake him quit of all the dark designs
That lure him to perdition ! Then shall she
Who loves him, maybe as *I* lov'd him once,
Hold to her heart once more a gentleman
Whose name shall blot no future hist'ry's page.
Yes, I will strive to ward aside the storm,
Nor perish in this light'ning flash of love !
> [*Writes hurriedly, and reads afterwards aloud.*

" I will do as you desire, so you bid farewell to treason ; and will join you on the ivy terrace, as the clock strikes ten."

[*Enter* GILES *as though to remove the supper.*]

ALICE.

Giles, you have ever been a trusty servant ;
See here this letter, 'tis for Mr. Babington—
Nay, I will even put his name upon it,
His new name sounding strange to me ; and hark,
See no one hath it saving Mr. Babington.

GILES.

He cross'd towards the stables as I pass'd,
Booted and spurr'd.   He doth not stay with us ?

ALICE (*in agitation*).

No—yes. (My brain seems reeling, and my words
Will tell my secret !)   No, he does not stay—
We do not stay.   Ah, Giles, think kindly of me !
God bless you, trusty Giles ; give me your hand.

GILES (*giving his hand, after first wiping it*).

A rough one, madam, but 'tis at your service.

ALICE.

Go now, and give the letter.   [*Exit.*

H 2

GILES.

Poor young lady !
Her head seems wand'ring !   Taking after him,
Our moody master !   He is wrong in the head,
Sure as my name is Giles.   Now for the letter—
" To   Mr.   Babington "   [*examining it*].   Ah,   Mr.
   Babington !
I mind me when we used to see you here,
Flesh days and fast days, sweet on Mistress Alice.
Methought one day I might have pledged your name
With hers in such a bumper as this here.
Now I must drink them singly ; howsomever,
The better plan for one who loves good liquor.

> [*Pours out goblet of wine, after first
> placing letter on table behind him.*

[*Enter* WILLOUGHBY, *who does not perceive* GILES.]

WILLOUGHBY (*to himself*).

Well, well—'tis for the best—'tis for the best.
Maybe 'twere foolishness to take a wife
In these unsettled times ; yet will I serve her,
And be her sworn true knight.   Aha ! the letter,

Which I had nigh forgotten, lately sealed
By that soft cruel hand !
> [*Taking possession of letter, after first
> kissing it. Reading over the direction.*
>   " To Mr. Babington."
Yes, yes, her mother's nephew.
>   [*Perceiving* GILES.
>   Ah, what now ?
When masters pray or slumber varlets drink.
On with my mantle for me.   Hast a lantern ?

GILES (*confused*).

A lantern ?—aye, a lantern—Mistress Alice——

WILLOUGHBY.

Make her my humble compliments, good Giles ;
Then to the stables ; whence I seek the village—
And so to London.

GILES (*aside*).

>   Out upon the letter !
Where hath it wing'd to ?

WILLOUGHBY.

>   Come, thou honest varlet !

[*Aside.*]   Yes, better not to see her—best to leave
   her
Silently, reverently, as a mem'ry
Of something sad and holy, gone for ever.
                              [*Exeunt into garden.*

[*Enter* ALICE *wrapped in a cloak.*]

ALICE (*nervously*).

Voices!   How anxiously my heart is beating!
'Tis not now ten o'clock, so Anthony
Waits me not yet.   I would that they would hasten—
If they should see him waiting!   Well, what matter,
So they guess not he waiteth there for me?
Alas! what dare I hope—what dare I pray for?
Success or failure?   For I seem to stand
Upon a dizzy height, with storms above;
Whilst at my feet a horrid precipice
Yawns to receive me!   [*Re-enter* GILES *from garden.*

GILES (*muttering to himself*).

A dang'rous time to travel, by my faith!
A foolish time to travel : but young heads
Are stronger than their elders'.

ALICE.

Think you so?
Nay, worthy Giles, the world is new to them,
With all its dangers.

GILES.

By your leave, my lady,
I think young heads will bear the hardest knocks,
And house more harmless bullets.   In mine own
There ran just now a silly old wife's tale
Of highway robbers ; how her goodman's hat
Had twenty shot-holes on that Easter-eve
The when she thought he had been fooling her
With village wantons.   So I said of the night,
"A dang'rous time to travel."

ALICE (*impatiently*).
Foolish tales !

GILES.
She hath the old hat still——

ALICE.

Nay, leave me now.
Your clatter deafens me—I have the vapours.

GILES.

For which, dear madam, take the head of a mole,
So it be caught towards the moon's decline,
And let it drip into a mug of beer
Brew'd on the birthday of some gentleman
Who owneth abbey lands——

ALICE.

Away, good Giles.
Methinks you too have drunk of some such brew.
Get thee to bed !

GILES.

'Tis true I drank his health
Ere he departed.

ALICE (*surprised*).

Is my cousin gone—
My cousin Willoughby—and no good-bye ?

GILES.

I heard him mutter it were better so.
He sent you, madam, his profound respects.

ALICE.

Well, well.   Now go.

GILES.

So, mistress, by your leave
(Forgive an old man who upon his knee
Hath ofttimes dandled you), two gentlemen
Of brave appearance, fearing man nor devil,
Will slink into the night like two kick'd curs,
For sake of two bright eyes; and yet, in sooth,
Who ever used to hold his head as high
As Mr. Babington?

ALICE (*in astonishment*).

How, Mr. Babington?

GILES.

He whom we thought would be our master here,
Only the wind blew wrong.   The Mr. Babington
That rides to-night to London.

ALICE.

Rides to London?

Where is he?

GILES.

On the road, and some way on,
With Colonel Willoughby—they ride together.
And so I said anon, like two kick'd curs,

Go from this house two gallant gentlemen,
Because of two bright eyes ; whilst of the night
I said (an' so it please you—by your leave),
A dang'rous time to travel.   Now I go.

ALICE (*eagerly*).

Not yet !   Not yet !   Ah, where is Anthony ?

GILES.

Poor Mr. Anthony !   He crosses now
The lone marsh lands betwixt us and the village,
With Colonel Willoughby.   They ride together
Alone and unattended, Peter Barton
Will only join them there.   I have known men
That rather would have broke their necks than ride
Alone and unattended by that way.

ALICE (*passionately*).

How, *gone ?*   So he could go, heart-whole and free,
And leave me ?—leave me seeming unto him
The thing my letter made me out to be ?—
A moth lured by the flicker of a love
Too fierce to ease the aching of this heart !
Oh heart !   why didst thou ache for such as he ?

Oh hand that wrote to him the words he scorn'd,
Thank God thou art not slave that wears his ring !
So I have bent me to the very earth,
And kiss'd those feet in fancy that have fled,
And left me crush'd and blushing and ashamed !
Ashamed ?   And wherefore should I be ashamed ?
Deem'd he I plann'd this all for love of him ?
For love of him who left me, loving once,
To wed another ?   Nay !   My love is dead !
This was for England !—this was for the queen
With half her nobles !   Whilst that Babington
Whose name shall blot our hist'ry's future page,
I know him not—he is not kin of mine—
He is forgotten ! [*Sobbing.*]   Oh, my heart is broken,
Now Anthony is gone !
                    [*Sinks towards a chair, half fainting.*

GILES (*supporting her*).

                              Ah, poor young lady !
Her mind is surely failing !   Poor young lady !

SCENE IV.—BABINGTON (*under the name of* BELLING-HAM) *and* COLONEL WILLOUGHBY *waiting under a tree, surrounded by a swamp, with reeds, &c., having lost their way. Horses tied up near.*

BABINGTON.

So now our hare-brained plan of riding seven miles in the dark meets its proper reward—nay, we do not even deserve this dry spot to rest upon, where I see nothing for it but to wait till daylight; for we can go neither backwards nor forwards in this damnable slough, and we have wandered some way off the road.

WILLOUGHBY.

Be of good courage, Mr. Bellingham. Methinks anon I heard voices and the clank of horsemen. We are not far off the beaten track.

BABINGTON.

Oh, it is not my courage that fails me, I was but laughing at our sorry plight ! Confess now, colonel though you be, that there are fires more enticing than those of these will-o'-the-wisps, and more terrible even than those of your Flanders campaign. Confess that it was the same cause made fools and cowards of us both ?

WILLOUGHBY (*sternly*).

How, sir, the same cause? And how cowards?
Most of all, how *coward?*

BABINGTON.

Oh, do not "sir" me. I am honest and out-
spoken, for a man may speak his mind in a morass.
Walls have ears, but your green duckweed and
black bulrush are safe listeners. It was Mistress
Alice drove us both out of house and home, and
lodged us here with such scant comfort. Confess,
colonel, you are as deep in love with her as our
bodies anon were plunged in this reeking quag-
mire !

WILLOUGHBY.

Every heart hath its own secrets, Mr. Bellingham;
and, without seeming squeamish to you, let me say
that the man who keeps these to himself is the
wisest. Who goes there?   [*Hearing voices.*

BABINGTON (*cocking his pistols*).

Who goes there?

> [*Masked figures advancing, armed;
> amongst them the traitor-servant of*
> BABINGTON.

1ST STRANGER.

Take him that called the other Bellingham !

2ND STRANGER.

Nay, take the one that was called Bellingham by the other.

3RD STRANGER.

We are robbers of the queen's highway. There is no escape. Deliver up your moneys and papers.

[WILLOUGHBY *overpowered by numbers,*
his pockets and saddle-bags rifled.

4TH STRANGER (*having discovered the letter addressed*
to BABINGTON *on* WILLOUGHBY).

This is our man, and now for a noble recompense.

2ND STRANGER.

" God prosper the harvest ! "

BABINGTON (*recognising the voice of* PETER BARTON).
Traitor !

[*Shoots him dead and escapes, leaving*
WILLOUGHBY *with the supposed*
robbers.

ACT III.

SCENE I.—*A guard-room at Tutbury Castle.* LORD SHREWSBURY, *holding in his hand* WALSINGHAM'S *letter. Messenger standing near a window looking into the grounds.*

SHREWSBURY (*muttering to himself*).

Strange ! there must be some deeper meaning in these words than meets my dull understanding. [*Reads.*] " Be not over stern with the Queen of Scots, now her health faileth. No need to restrain her to the leads, if she can take the air in the gardens ;" and then these words afterwards—" But keep close watch on her morning, noon, and night." If 'tis to trap her I will be no party to it, for she must lull herself with no hope of a false security. Heigho ! what with these two queens and mine own she-devil, life is but a sorry pastime !

MESSENGER (*advancing*).

Is there no way, my lord, by which I might have sight of the queen ere I return to London? Doth she ever use these gardens? So I might but see her pass I should be content. A right royal lady still, I hear.

SHREWSBURY.

No doubt but what meets the eye is that which pleaseth most in her, and this I say after some acquaintance; and yet much of the beauty of this queen is bought, aye, and as yet unpaid for.

MESSENGER.

But will she pass into the garden?

SHREWSBURY.

She hath been abed for the last five days, pleading an abscess in her neck, and this, with the swelling of her legs, hath made my work easier; yet not one of these things can be sworn to, for, you must know, she hath her own physician. Now, this is the way with this queen, she will lie in bed eight days at a stretch, sometimes denying herself to all comers, untired and slovenly, after the manner of the French, and looking (as I am told by my lady) double her age when bereft of those dyes and pigments that so help her beauty.

MESSENGER.

My lord, you are somewhat hard on her majesty.

SHREWSBURY (*continuing*).

At other times she will sit arrayed in all that she hath of her best—and she hath gewgaws enow in all conscience, seeing that now we are moving from Tutbury she demandeth eighty waggons to carry them. At these times she will see those that are allowed audience of her, eating with them, or playing games with dice or draughts on the coverlid of her bed, and entertaining them with lively talk. I hear that she hath entertained embassies in this fashion in Scotland, and this, coupled with her extravagance and her adulteries, so outraged the rough Scots that it lost her her kingdom!

MESSENGER (*smiling*).

You are, indeed, merciless, my lord, to what many deem only the pretty failings of woman!

I

SHREWSBURY.

Nay, nay ; I am but just. There is much in her
that is neither pretty nor womanly, but she hath some
great qualities. Lesser at times than a woman,
there are moments when she rises above the mental
height of a man ; and could Langside have been won
by courage and despising of fatigue, she had not
now been here—nor I either, God help me !

MESSENGER.

Is any of this old courage remaining to her?

SHREWSBURY.

At times, when suddenly rising, she will order
saddle-horses, and hunt and hawk one day after
another, making the limbs of the ladies of her
following to ache for a week. How they endure
it I marvel. But her chiefest virtue is to endear
to her those about her immediate person. Though
'tis, peradventure, but the calculation of a selfish
nature, to insure that they leave no whim ungratified.

MESSENGER (*smiling*).

I may, at any rate, report, my lord, that you are
a most loyal subject of our queen's, and that you
will say not one good word of her rival, your

whimsical captive. One of these said whims may take her majesty to the garden. With your permission I will stroll there for awhile, whilst your lordship prepares your answer to my papers.

SHREWSBURY.

My lens is set to focus her at a wise distance. Neither am I so near her as to be under her glamour, nor so far as but to judge her by the noise of an inflamed and scurrilous report. I see her as she *is*—a princess of high courage, but a woman and a *liar*.

MESSENGER.

All great princes should know the diplomatic art of lying. *Our* queen can lie !

SHREWSBURY (*aside*).

Aye, but badly. This queen will lie against her and beat her.

MESSENGER.

Nevertheless I would fain see her. I await your summons in the garden.

> [*Exit* MESSENGER, *leaving* SHREWSBURY *plunged in thought, and again reading paper.*

I 2

SCENE II.—*An apartment at Tutbury Castle.* MARY
STUART *reclining on a sofa in a loose robe. Enter*
MARY BEATON, *her attendant.*

MARY BEATON.

Your majesty did call?

QUEEN.

Yes. I would rise
And tire me in my best, I have a boon
To ask my lord, my gaoler.

MARY BEATON.

Which same boon,
Being a member of the one true faith
(Unlike the heretic churl we parted from,
Without much waste of weeping), he will grant,
I feel assured, dear madam.

QUEEN.

I less sure.

MARY BEATON.

What! seeing you, sweet madam, plead to him,
All tired to conquer better men than he?

QUEEN.

Your Scotch and English are a race of churls,
Unlike the light French lords ; to Shrewsbury
I seem no better than this chair or table,
(I say this truth in all humility).
To him methinks all women seem alike.

MARY BEATON (*smiling*).

Yet there be chairs and chairs, and so with tables—
He knoweth rich from homely furniture,
And gold from pewter !

QUEEN (*sadly*).

These are such gloomy, chill, imprison'd days,
I sometimes wonder they have left me life
Worth counting living !   You must wonder too ?

MARY BEATON.

I wonder at nothing now !   All wonderment
Is dead in me.   Your highness's brief years
Have been so fill'd with all astonishment.

QUEEN.

Ah, not so brief ! my night is closing in.
Ah, Mary, could we wend to some warm shore
Smiling to greet us !   I have read such tales

Of sweet Italian places by blue seas,
I long to seek them! Could we drink in life
And great glad sunlight under olive trees
Gray, with their gnarled trunks, their dreamy shade,
Like vapour meeting skies serene and blue,
Which flush to rosier light at eventide
Behind the black sharp furthest mountain-ridge,
There citrons hang upon the burden'd bough,
Or flow'r to waft a challenge of defiance
Towards the crowding violets, as jealous
Of which should smell the sweetest! Think on this,
And then behold yon fest'ring lichens creep
Amongst the slimy cresses on that pond,
See yon starved robin pecking at a worm
Amongst the clinging furrows deep with clay,
And listen to the wind that beats the smoke
Adown this dismal chimney: yet forsooth
They call this spring-tide! All my weary soul
Is longing for the South!

MARY BEATON.

                    The while I deemed
Your heart, dear madam, hungered for the North.
Methought your royal spirit sought the shore

Of pine-clad Denmark, where Lord Bothwell bides.
And yet 'tis cold in Denmark, is it not?
There blow methinks the dread north winds of heaven,
Let loose like sleuth hounds on their track that flee
From slow despair. This had I thought, dear madam.

QUEEN.

Ah! I would take my north wind to the South,
And hold it to my bosom till its breath
Breathed life into me, whilst without the world
Thaw'd to the warm midsummer of my love.
Oh, Mary, there was never love like this—
A bold north love, sun-scented with the south!

MARY BEATON.

Ah! may your highness bask in such a love—
May it come to you with the crown o' the realm!

QUEEN (*sadly*).

It may come to me with a martyr's crown,
Strive not to dupe me who am now no child,
My bold north love is o'er, Bothwell is dead!
                                        [*Weeps.*

MARY BEATON.

Nay, madam, you are gloomy. Have good courage!

QUEEN (*continuing*).

Ah, child, you deem these days have left me shorn
Of all my bygone buoyancy of mind ?
How long, ye saints, must I, Christ's handmaid, wait
For freedom or for glory in a world
Where these base elements wherefrom I groan
Exist not ?
            You will wonder at the change
So lately come to one of my proud blood.
Doubtless you deem I lose my spirit's fire
Stifled amidst the cold, and damp, and squalor
Of this our prison-house, wherein the rains
Drip thro' the mould'ring ceilings, whilst the winds
Rattle the crazy casements, where the owl,
The bat-mouse, and the noisome dunghill rat
Are fellow-sojourners with Scotland's queen !

MARY BEATON.

Yet now your highness knows all this is past.
Since we are bound ere long to Chartley Manor.

QUEEN.

Past ! Yea, my transient gleam of sun is past,
But not the coming evil of new days !
Sometimes I deem my race is doom'd to ill.

When have we thriven ?   'Twere too long to tell
Of plot and counter-plot, risings in arms,
Not even like yon chess-board, black with white
Alternate, knew my inoffensive years
Storm and fine weather—sorrow, always black ;
The poor bright squares of happiness so rare
Mere white surprises on the growing dark !

MARY BEATON.

Ah, madam, you are fanciful to-day !

QUEEN.

Nay, nay, not fanciful, but truthful, child.
Think how I throve amidst a storm of hail—
My mother and the cardinal at war
With hydra-headed heresies.   Remember
How these two struggled to exterminate
The hornet-horde of heretics !   Remember
The man that nail'd the ram's horns on St. Francis,
And then the impious Wishart—thought of these
Kindles my blood so hot that it could burn them !

MARY BEATON.

Calm yourself, madam, they were burnt on earth,
And now burn on for ever !

QUEEN.

Calm is past.
Come storm—come anything save this dead life !
Come change, come turmoil ! Nay, I hug my wrongs,
Since now I hope the near accomplishment
Of God's just vengeance on His enemies,
And mine, and yours ! Ah, can you hear of them
Seeming unmoved, as now ?—and you a Beaton,
Blood of the murder'd cardinal !

MARY BEATON.

Ah, madam,
You seem'd to have forgotten this till now,
With half your wrongs, and e'en Lord Bothwell's
    death.

QUEEN (*continuing, excitedly*).
You deem this crush'd me, child—yea, for awhile
Such dealing chill'd my blood, and seemed to sink
My mind unto a swoon-like apathy,
Killing the queen within me, who became
Naught but an ailing woman. This is o'er,
And with the first return of health and spring
I feel the couchant tiger in my blood
Arise refresh'd, as having slept awhile,

And thereby gained new suppleness and force :
I thirst for vengeance ! Let them guard her well,
Their queen ! And have I written with this hand,
Calling her " my good sister ?" She shall rue
The day when she held prisoner in her land
One of the old Stuart stock ! Hast ever seen
A pictured semblance of the king of beasts
Bound down with cords, which at the under' side
A little mouse is gnawing with his teeth ?
Either I dream, or, too elate with hope,
I meet my wish too far this side its end ;
Or else—(nay, child, maybe I only dream !)—
Some little mouse is gnawing at my chain.

MARY BEATON.

God grant it, madam, and that he break not his
teeth !

[*Enter* SERVANT.]

SERVANT.

Lord Shrewsbury craves permission to speak with
your highness.

QUEEN.

We wait him. Let him enter.

[*Enter* LORD SHREWSBURY.]

SHREWSBURY (*bowing low, but not looking the* QUEEN
in the face).

　　　　　　　　Do I find
Your majesty restored to health again ?

QUEEN (*coaxingly*).
An you would deign to raise your eyes, my lord,
Perchance you might observe that this poor face
Wears trace of coming summer.　These new winds
Bringing these moister mornings, fill our lungs
Less harshly than that piercing pain of weather
Before the rains.　'Twere sweet to wander now,
Breathing the scent of May-buds satisfied
That thirsted for this rain.

SHREWSBURY.
　　　　　　　　This may not mean
Your majesty would walk abroad to-day ?
Your majesty who some few days ago
Bewail'd yourself, talking of rheumatism,
With agues, faintings, water in the blood—
Deeming these dire distempers all begot
Of English damp and English prison fare—
So hath your majesty misnamed the diet

With which we strive to flatter, if may be,
Your majesty's fine palate, used, no doubt,
To Frenchmen's food.   We Englishmen are rougher,
Perchance—I do not know, but yet methinks
I, standing here, well reach'd my middle age,
Could tackle your ten Frenchmen !

QUEEN.

Nay, my lord,
You ever seem to fly off " hunting hares,"
As we who chased the red deer used to say
Long since in Scotland, when it chanced some hound,
Mistaking passing accident for purpose,
Scented the lesser quarry.   And, again,
Whene'er you have your fling at Frenchmen's fare,
At Frenchmen's cut of clothes or cut of beard,
We notice that your lady and yourself
Will look at us askance.   Nay, by the rood !
We think, my lord (forgive us for our speech),
On one thing only are you two agreed—
To flaunt us for a Frenchwoman !

SHREWSBURY (*coldly*).

Nay, madam,
You surely wrong me.   As for Lady Shrewsbury

I will not answer—nay, I wash my hands
Of Lady Shrewsbury !

QUEEN.

What ! of your own wife !
And you a Catholic ?   Out, out upon you !
We needs must school you who are 'neath your rule,
My Lord of Shrewsbury!   Then, as for Frenchwoman,
After the queen's decease (whom God defend),
Where lives there in the land one, like ourself,
Uniting nearest blood with truest faith—
The one true faith—your faith, my lord, and mine ?

SHREWSBURY.

Nay, madam, these are subjects I eschew !
I know my duty to my sovereign lady,
And may I know it at a later day
If (as some hope who serve your majesty)
The crown she wears pass to another's brow ;
But now I will not parley of such chance.
Yet I, who seem to you a blunt, rough man,
Have yet some forethought of your highness's weal,
And so I would advise you, should you walk
Or ride abroad to-day, between the rains,
To have a care, and mind you that those watch

Your grace's movements who are bound to do it
From lealty to their queen, to whom myself
Am likewise bounden, thus to do her service,
Yet to you, madam, would I, too, be faithful,
And so I warn your highness.   .

QUEEN (*to* MARY BEATON, *aside*).
                              Can he mean
Those watch for me as some now watch for her,
To do me bodily harm?   Nay, nay, not thus
Would she best clear her kingdom of my claims !
Nay !   I defy her malice !
                    [*Aloud to* LORD SHREWSBURY.
                              Then my lord
Gives his permission that we walk abroad ?

SHREWSBURY.
Yes ; I am blunt, and so forgive my words.
I give permission not of my free will ;
'Tis that I have her majesty's commands
To deal more leniently with your highness.
Of my free will I had not seem'd so kind,
Deeming no good can come unto your highness,
Of long duration, whilst at liberty
To foster madmen's dreams, who make your name

A pass-word for their treasons.   This will be
Unknown e'en to yourself, whilst men may say
" The Queen of Scots can take her walks abroad,"
" The Queen of Scots may mark this sign or that."
Yet, madam, let the Queen of Scots remember
The Queen of England hath her at her bidding,
And see she proves her worthy of the trust
Which makes that queen (for what good, heaven   knoweth !)
Deal softly with her !   I have said my say,
I make your highness my obeisance.   [*Exit.*

QUEEN.

What think you, Mary, means that exhortation ?
It somehow seemed half sermon and half threat,
And yet it had in it a ring of friendship,—
I cannot fathom it.

MARY BEATON.

                        He seemed to speak
Almost as nurses chide a wilful child,
Saying " Thou shalt not, or thou shalt repent."
Oh ! that your highness should thus suffer wrong
To your high queenly dignity !

QUEEN.

Hush, child !
We have borne deeper wrongs, and it may be
Our gaoler is an honest man at heart,
The which may bleed for us ; or else perchance
His lady, like the tiger-cat she is,
May have aspersed us to him, who at us
Hurls the ill-humour he is forced to hide
From her keen eye that rules him.   All ends well
Seeing our boon is granted, and these feet
(So falt'ring now !) may tread, between the rains,
Those garden-glades, and these lips breathe the balm
For which they thirst, of spring-buds satisfied !

[MARY BEATON *helps the* QUEEN *on with her mantle.*
The QUEEN *herself, stooping, puts on her shoes.*

MARY BEATON (*in horror*).
Nay, madam, not the left ! the right foot first
Let me withdraw it, and thus break the spell !

QUEEN.
That would but hinder me.   What is the hour ?

MARY BEATON.
Five o' the clock ; remember, prithee, madam,
The harm that for like foolish act assail'd

K

The Emperor Augustus, for 'tis writ—

> " Augustus having by oversight
> Put on his left shoe before his right,
> Was like to have been slain next day
> By soldiers mutinying for pay."

QUEEN.

We risk no such mischance, who have no army
To mutiny, nor pay to satisfy;
So let the shoe stay on, and get thee cloak'd
And bonneted to bear me company.

SCENE III.—*A terraced garden with an ivied wall.
Shrubs near it, amongst which.* WALSINGHAM'S
MESSENGER *conceals himself on hearing the*
QUEEN *and* MARY BEATON.

MESSENGER (*aside*).

A goodly lady, eyes that might have graced
The brows of Egypt's queen ; a royal air,
And such a voice as leads men to their doom.
At last these eyes have seen the Queen of Scots,
She that hath made such turmoil in the land !

QUEEN (*to* MARY BEATON).

This is the place, here where the bulging buttress
Doth seem as though it totter'd.   Here, to-day,
If friends are lurking near, I shall behold
A handful of gray pebbles from the sea
Scatter'd amongst the ivy.   They are here.
Now was I bade to droop in careless wise
Over the masonry, as tho' to scan
The distant landscape.   One will come 'ere long,
Who, climbing up the shadow'd side of wall,
Will slip into my hanging hand the cyphers,
Telling if all goes well.   If seen by any,
Well, 'tis some yokel who hath made a vow
To see the Queen of Scots and touch her hand,
For the king's evil.   He will act the clown
To those who set upon him.   You will watch,
And at the sound of coming voice or footfall,
Trill gently that old song I made in France.
Now leave me, Mary.

MESSENGER (*aside*).
                    Ha ! it seems to me
I witness some conspiracy.   Strange chance !
Now to observe and listen.

QUEEN (*hearing someone on the other side of the
wall, over which she is leaning*).
Is't a friend ?

Voice of BABINGTON.
A friend who sayeth from his inmost heart,
" God speed the harvest."

QUEEN.
Babington himself !
Our page at Sheffield. We had known your face
Amongst a thousand ! For all service done
And doing for us, we desire to thank you.
We are alone, so you are free to speak.

BABINGTON (*showing himself, disguised as a rustic*).
Madam, my most dread sov'reign and my liege,
To this dear moment hath my wingèd hope
Travell'd till now unbless'd. I kneel, abash'd,
Before my one anointed queen of queens ! [*Kneels.*

QUEEN.
Arise our truest friend, nor kneel to one
So fetter'd and abased : in all your land
There bides no beggar is as poor as we—
Bereft by sland'rous tongues of honour, crown,

(We mourn for honour first), nay *crowns*, my friend—
Bereft of all we women-folk hold dear.
Rise, Babington, nor kneel to such an one—
Yet could these few poor unconsider'd words
Of broken English—(it is hard your tongue) —
Tell you but faintly all our thanks to you
And those your brave companions, we could speak
Indefinitely.   Time encroaches, friend,
Give us the cyphers.   Ah ! and not so changed
As when our pretty page !   [*Strokes his cheek.*

   [BABINGTON *kisses her hand and gives the cyphers,*
       which the QUEEN *conceals in her sleeve.*

QUEEN (*scornfully*).
                And so they thought
To cage for ever in their cobweb cage
A Queen of Scotland and a Queen of France !

BABINGTON.
Madam, a Queen of *England*—prais'd be God !
Some noble hearts beat only to that end.

QUEEN.
We thank those noble hearts, and bid them beat
Till our sad heart cease beating.   There is hope

Whilst life thus thro' this somewhile tortured frame
Flows without sign of flinching.   Fare you well !

BABINGTON.

Your highness leaves me happiest of slaves.
Like Moses, may the glory of my face
Illuminate the souls of those who *wait.*
Adieu my dear liege-lady !   [*Kissing both her hands.*

QUEEN.

Fare you well !

[MARY BEATON *is heard singing in the distance, to
warn the* QUEEN *of approaching footsteps.*

ACT IV.

Scene I.—(*Some months are supposed to have elapsed since last Act*). *The oak room at* Jerome Bel-lamy's. Alice and Willoughby *in conversation*.

Willoughby.

Oh it is all out! and it is as infernal a plot as ever the Evil One put into the mind of a man to imagine. It has run through the whole of England as swiftly as the distempered blood flows through the veins of one that is bitten of a mad dog, another moment and it had attained the heart.

Alice.

It is all most terrible!

Willoughby.

Besides the queen's death and the Spanish invasion,

ít is discovered that they have held communications as concerning the sacking of the City of London ; they had devised to rob some of the richest men in England, to fire the ships, and to cloy all the great ordnance—and all this to bring back the Pope ! If this is their *Religio Catholica*, 'twere better had they christened it *Diabolica*. But *you*, of course, are well informed of all this !

ALICE.

Wherefore am I so well informed ? It hath all been to me as some horrible dream !

WILLOUGHBY.

Because (and my heart bleeds when I say to you these words) your own cousin is at the head of this plot—that Anthony Babington, for whom you gave me this letter—your mother's nephew—*your* cousin but not mine, I thank heaven !

ALICE *(in agitation)*.

Where did you get this letter ? Its seal is broken —who has read it ?

WILLOUGHBY.

Four sham freebooters, who tore it from my breast on the night when, you may mind you, you said (laying your hand thus on my leathern jerkin), "Place it there," and there it was they found it. I shall never forget that your hand was there——

ALICE.

When did this happen?

WILLOUGHBY.

Months ago now, after our last sad meeting. Since then the plot hath been so surging and thickening around us, we have had our hands and ·minds full, I warrant you. After all they were no freebooters, but some of our queen's party on the look out for traitors. It seems Peter Barton, a servant of Babington's, had turned queen's evidence, and was on the look out, deeming, no doubt, when he came into these parts that, as he was your kinsman, he would be your guest. This ruffian was shot by Mr. Bellingham, my travelling companion, who took him for the robber he seemed, and I had afterwards some trouble in proving their error to those that had hold of me, as, having on me a letter for him, and the darkness somewhat hiding my features, they took my grizzled locks for a wig, and my sturdier frame for borrowed flesh, for it seems he hath many disguises, being sometimes arrayed as a soldier, a rustic, an Abraham-man, or a Tom o' Bedlam, and so would have it until daylight that I was Babington and no other.

ALICE.

And Mr. Bellingham?

WILLOUGHBY.

He was off across the bleak moorland like a roe-deer. One had said he fear'd for his life had he not seem'd hitherto a gallant young gentleman— nor since then have I heard of him.

ALICE.

Nor I either ; and these men read my letter?

WILLOUGHBY.

These men read your letter, and, throwing it back to me, said it was only from some foolish wench who was sweet on the traitor, tho' they said it proved his treasons without doubt, in that his sweet-heart prayed him to desist from them. So this was the man you lov'd !—a traitor—a renegade—one who would have compassed the queen's death !

ALICE.

Ah cousin, spare me !

WILLOUGHBY.

It was for *him* that as a thing of naught you
set aside the love of an honest man—for the sake
of one whose name will be for ever a slur on his
old house—and a byword for the whole of loyal
England to scoff at!

ALICE.

I will not answer you; my lips are sealed. You
are speaking at random, knowing no more who is
the man I have loved than you know now where
is that Babington at whom you are jeering.

WILLOUGHBY.

Ha! I do not know where he is? Am I so
far from suspecting his whereabouts? Why, then,
am I here? Did I come once more to madden
myself with your scorn of my love? Nay! I obeyed
but the voice of a stern necessity which bids me
search this house in the queen's name. *Anthony
Babington is in this house.*

ALICE.

In this house? Nay, you are speaking, indeed, at
random!

WILLOUGHBY.

Thank God if I am, Alice. I would not for worlds that Anthony Babington were found in this house; for if he is here it is that as is suspected—your uncle is one of his accomplices. And though, if he leave as my prisoner, he is a doomed man (since out of the loyalty that I owe the queen I will not that he escape), and though you once said to me that whilst he lived you would wed "no other living man," still, such is the folly of love, Alice, that though I answered then, "Would that he were dead," I say now, "Would heaven I may not bring him to his death, would heaven I could save him!"

ALICE (*bitterly*).

And yet you would not that he escape you? Such is the love of a man!

WILLOUGHBY.

Such is the duty of a soldier to his queen. Then he *is* here? I pray'd this had not been!

ALICE (*excitedly*).

Ah! now I have it! All is as plain as day. My grandfather's will left me my uncle's heir if I should wed a Protestant and found a family professing the new religion. You are my guardian, my kinsman, and a Protestant to boot, a soldier, and one trusted of the queen. With all this you might hold high junketing in London and at Court had you but the wherewithal—but this, you have said, will come in marrying me. This is your boasted love ; this is why you come to me now, my heart bleeding for my poor kinsman, my playmate, my childhood's friend—and tell me he is doomed to die, that a price is set on his head, and that he is a regicide, a traitor, and a disgrace to his old house !

WILLOUGHBY.

Calm yourself, Alice ; you are unjust. [*Aside.*] Ah, this was then really the man she loved !

ALICE.

You hope for his death ! You hope for my uncle's attainder ! These two out of your path, and, you have said, "I shall gain two things"—by which you meant, a rich wife and the death of one you thought she had loved ; forby, if my uncle dies, and I am wedded to you, a Protestant, I am his heir—his heir and your wife, as you think. You think these old

elm trees, crowned with their crow colonies, will
bow their heads to you and own you for master.
You are mistaken.   You are blind.   You do not
know.   No, no, never! never!   Each sighing tree
would seem a wailing ghost to you.   All these
pictures would scowl at you from under their beetle
brows.   These creaking wainscots would sound as
the grating laughter of fiends.   At midnight *his* white
face would haunt you, whilst everything, alive or
dead, from roof to basement, from the song of the
first sad bird at dawn to the croak of the black rook
that comes home last from the fields at eventide,
would hiss at you the same words, "Anthony Babington is gone, and it was you that brought him to
his death!"   [*Weeps.*

WILLOUGHBY.

Then Babington is here in hiding?   And I, with
my great love for you, must deal you this blow.

ALICE.

I swear he is not here.   He is no more here than
your love.   I have found the key-note to your love!

WILLOUGHBY.

My poor child, you know not what you are saying.

The loyal soldier who weds with the daughter or niece of a traitor hath to swallow much that is not to his liking; though this one who loves her will readily do. If Anthony Babington is found in this house it is true that he is a dead man, and so far out of my way if he is the man who stood between us. But this fact will prove your uncle is of the plot. He will suffer with Babington. His goods will be forfeited to the Crown, and you are a pauper and homeless; and so I say, not for myself but for you, pray Heaven we find no traitors in this house.

ALICE.

I will swear to you, by all that I hold sacred, he is not here !

Enter unperceived JEROME BELLAMY *and* FATHER HARINGTON.]

BELLAMY (*aside to* HARINGTON).

Did I not say that. you may always trust a woman to lie ?

WILLOUGHBY (*continuing*).

I will take your word, cousin Alice ; and though my warrant obliges me to search the house and the woods surrounding it, you may be sure I shall in no way abuse me of so undesired an authority.

ALICE.

Thank you, cousin ; and I crave your forgiveness if any of my bitter words wounded your kind heart. I have been well-nigh beside myself since this bad news.

WILLOUGHBY.

I will not let this stand between what you would call our friendship, Alice. [*Perceiving* BELLAMY.] Kinsman, I have a sad duty to perform. I hold here a warrant to search your house for some traitors who are known to be harboured in this neighbour-hood. They have doubled, like foxes, and you must not marvel if your religion, coupled with your kinship to this Babington, maketh it suspected that he may be here.

BELLAMY (*ironically*).

Sir, you have but your duty to perform. Go, search every nook and corner of this poor dwelling. See, here are the keys of every chamber, and those that are unlocked you will be free to enter. In one you will find my agèd mother in her bed, upon

whom all these dire tidings have fallen as a bolt
from heaven. Spare her gray head as much as you
can of what must needs bow it to the dust! This
worthy Father [*pointing to the priest*], who has been
for many years my counsellor and spiritual guide,
desires that he escape not the humiliations that have
been heaped upon others of his cloth. He desires,
nay, he *demands*, that you search him, as also the
chamber in which he is lodged. Nay, tear aside
his soutane and look that beneath it he doth not
wear trunk hose. Mark well the cut of his tonsure.
See, he has bared his white hairs——

WILLOUGHBY (*embarrassed*).

Nay, cousin, you both wound and embarrass me!
—this is a sad duty.

BELLAMY (*continuing*).

Here, sir, is my library or study [*opens a door to
left*]—here where it is my habit to write. Search
each paper and document, nay, look well betwixt
the leaves of each old book, and see that you
examine the fittings of the wainscot. To the left
there are situate my kitchens, larders, and outhouses,
not forgetting the wood-lofts and hay-ricks, for 'tis

L

a common trick of your conspirators to hide amongst hay or faggots. Here are my serving men and maids who are at present lingering over their ale [*opening a door to right*]. Look well at each one of them. Rise, varlets, and pull your forelocks to the gentleman who is searching the house in the name of the queen! [*Servants discovered at supper.*

WILLOUGHBY (*scarcely looking at the servants assembled*).

You are hard on me, cousin!

ALICE.

Uncle, you are hard on cousin Nicholas, who wishes us no ill!

WILLOUGHBY.

God knows I do not, and I heartily trust my search may prove unsuccessful. Have I your permission to do my sad duty? I search first the house and then the gardens and grounds.

BELLAMY.

Assuredly, sir; and lest it be thought we go but to throw dust in your eyes, neither myself nor any of my family shall accompany you.

[*Exit* WILLOUGHBY.

[*Triumphantly, as soon as he has departed.*]
Aye, blockhead, go and search among stocks and stones for the man who stood anon but three paces from you ! Go into byre and barn, and turn over the straw in the horses' stall. You will not find him. Anthony Babington is here !

[*Enter* BABINGTON, BARNWELL, *and* DONN, *disguised as rustics, from room to the right.*]

ALICE (*in horror*).
What, here ! Anthony here ! Great God, what will become of us !

BABINGTON.
Thanks to you all for helping us to outwit that short-sighted swashbuckler. These are my two friends, Mr. Robert Barnwell and Mr. Henry Donn; but for you [*turning to* BELLAMY] we had all been in a sorry plight.

ALICE (*in alarm*).
Back, then, to your place of hiding, for the love of heaven, since you *are* here !

BABINGTON.
Not till I have pledged you all in this bumper,

L 2

and drank the health of our sovereign lady the queen.
[*Raising glass.*]   Long live Queen Mary!

WILLOUGHBY (*entering unperceived*).

Nay, long live Queen Elizabeth! Anthony Babington, Robert Barnwell, and Henry Donn, I arrest
you in the name of the queen's majesty! [*Aside.*]
Though would to heaven some other man had the
doing of this deed!

[*Enter soldiers, servants, &c.*]

ACT V.

SCENE I.—*A room in the Tower very early in the morning.* ALICE *and* BABINGTON.

ALICE (*sadly*).

How do we meet? Would heaven I had died,
Nor seen you thus ! My heart lies dead in me
For very sorrow !

BABINGTON.

All things have an end :
So end my dreams. As man must one day die,
What matter whether 'tis at chilly Yule
Or warm midsummer ? 'Tis but as some journey
Which fate predestin'd me to undertake
A day or two before ; years seem but hours
To those who gaze mistrustfully at Time,

Failing to clip his wings. The happy years,
Men say, fly fastest. I, who ne'er have stoop'd
To wallow in that paradise of fools
Wherein some seem contented, scarcely know
The common meaning of that common thing
Which men call happiness. I nursed my hopes,
And these are fled. What matter when I die?

ALICE.

You are resigned, poor cousin, prais'd be God!
May He sustain you to the bitter end.
I know you had firm courage and resolve.

BABINGTON.

These things are only letters strung together,
Nor know we wholly of what stuff we are,
Until we reach that end of which you speak,
Calling it bitter. But whether bitter or sweet,
There is a stronger force than firm resolve—
The force that leads the rack'd one to declare
Himself a guilty man, whose hands are clean,
Or their hands bloody that were once his friends.
This force is *Pain*. And those that best endure
First, thought of this, and after, pain itself—

Stand out the bravest men in history.
And yet 'tis not their mental probity
They forfeit, as their straining sinews wince
Under accumulating torture.   See,
I dash this hardware vessel to the ground,
        [*Throws earthen platter on the ground.*
It stands the shock, nor splinters in the fall ;
Yet dared I try with such a feeble thing
As seems some egg-shell brought you over sea,
It would be lost to you—in fifty bits.
'Tis but the clay that is not staunch enough, ⎸
And whose fault, save the potter's ?   So with us—
The brave soul prison'd in the porcelain shell,
Shrinks thro' its agony of fibre and nerve,
The better borne by him of stouter frame,
E'en were he craven-hearted.   Thus it is—
And whose fault save the potter's ?

ALICE.
                None the less,
My dear, dear love that was (I call you thus,
Knowing you never may be love of mine),
You will not swerve in your fidelity
To those that were your friends ? Nay, should the rack,

Accursed engine ! (Ah, can God's just eye
Look on and see it?) torture your poor frame,
(Too horrid thought !) set your teeth thus, and thus
Let your nails gnaw into your clenching palms,
Rather than speak ! Nay, drag your aching limbs
Like our old kinsman rack'd under King Harry,—
But do not e'er betray them ! Promise me !

BABINGTON.

But for the parable I made anon,
Of hardware and poor porcelain, I would promise.

ALICE.

See, I am made of porcelain, since I fall,
And falling, break ; and broken, cease to be
A thing of any worth ! Here, read this letter,
And see how I had fallen for your sake,
That you might rise the stronger to subdue
The powers of evil !

       [Shows the letter she had written to him.

BABINGTON.

      Ha ! you would have gone
With me, your evil genius, to perdition ?
Yes, I believ'd it, and so counted strange
Your obstinate refusal, since till then

I seemed to lead mankind ; I know not wherefore,
Nor wholly whither, yet I had a mission,
Methinks, to influence the mass of men,
So wonder'd at a woman like yourself
Saying me nay so stoutly ; ne'ertheless
You *would* have gone had I not gone the first.
History will know me as a leader of· men !

ALICE (*sorrowfully*).
A leader ? a deluder of yourself,
Whilst those who lov'd you followed in your track.
Yes, Anthony, this had I done for you
And love of something that seem'd once like love,
Yet heaven will'd it otherwise.

BABINGTON (*tenderly*).
Poor child,
And so you lov'd me !

ALICE.
What was once my love
Methinks I could not help but love a little,
Tho' only as a spirit hovers o'er
Some memory of earth.   Betwixt us two
Naught could arise that would not seem a ghost,

A guilty shrinking phantom ! You are married ;
How may I serve your wife ?

BABINGTON.

You are an angel,
Which, had I known the earlier, man nor devil
Had lured me from you ! My unhappy wife
Knows naught of this, but nursing on her knee
Her child so soon left desolate, oft looks,
I doubt not, at the noisy ticking clock
In the old home in Derbyshire. (The clock
That notes weeks, months, and changes of the moon,
The which these eyes of mine may note no more !)
And listens for a step that cometh not.
I have been traitor to her love and yours !

ALICE.

I will go to her, set your mind at rest.
And afterwards——Ah, God ! it breaks my heart
To think of afterwards !

> [*Covers her face with her hands.*

BABINGTON.

You will be friend and comforter to her.
And you will whisper to my hapless child
Pointing towards the radiance of the sun)

" I once knew one who strove to scale blue heaven
To grasp some such far glory, and who fell
· The lower that he strove to climb so high."

ALICE.

Dare I to look upon the face of one,
Your child and yet not mine, some such sad words
I'll say to him, so I can school my voice,
Remembering his father.

BABINGTON.

Thank you, Alice.
You seem an angel on the earth, and yet
Your acts die with you, like mere ashes and dust ;
Mine will live after me, tho' lamentable,
Bearing no blossom, blighted in the bud,
Still, men will speak of me.

ALICE.

And this was then,
Poor cousin, your high glory, grasping which
You fell to earth, that worms might blate of worms.
A small ambition !

BABINGTON.

Nay, I know this now—
Or partly know it—once it seem'd good cheer

To think that men should name me after death.
Blowing my trumpet with fine flourish of praise.
But now, I fear me, nothing brings good cheer
To deaf gray ashes lying under ground.

ALICE.

Except God's grace.

BABINGTON.

E'en this comes not to us,
As in the memorable days of old
Unto the saints.   Vainly, in these sad times,
We wait the guiding-finger from on high.
That faith should live at all, I marvel me.
And yet mine flourish'd fresh and green till now.

ALICE.

I pray that it may flourish to the end.

BABINGTON.

" The end ! "   Is this the end—the bitter end ?

ALICE.

Nay, the beginning of a better life.   [*Sobbing.*

BABINGTON.

Thus this life ends, as other men begin
To spin a tangled spider's web of errors,
Wherein to trap themselves !   *My* web is wove.

New aspirations, new astonishments,
New desolation !

> ALICE.
> Yes, new desolation—

Tho' mostly to the desolate who *wait*—
Seeing but emptiness where once was life,
With hope and promise of long prosp'rous years !

> BABINGTON.

After me, Alice, shall come other men.
There will be births and deaths throughout the earth,
With constant sound of merry marriage-bells,
And solemn-sounding requiems ; but these
(The ringing in and out of human kind,
E'en in the space that should have been my day)
I shall not hear.   A dead man lying deaf,
Or hearing other music !   Not for me
Will Spring's winds blow, to scatter wantonly
White rings of hawthorn blossom on the sward,
As Summer glows to meet her !   Yet all these
Have never seem'd so fair to me as now.
Time was, I did not value them enough,
And now, time is to leave them.   Unto you,
And these, farewell !   Maybe such things wax small

Before God's promise.   I shall know ere long,
Yet may not come to tell you.

ALICE.

One thing more—
The letter that you were to write the queen,
Suing for pardon?

BABINGTON.

I have not the heart,
The courage, or the cowardice to write it.
And then of what avail?   Here in the dark,
The vision of my blinded intellect
Seems quicken'd, like the keen eyes of a cat,
To see the things that heretofore were hid.
I see for future safety to the realm,
The queen must hang me.

ALICE.

Nay, the queen is kind,
I hear that what we common-folk consider
Her alternations, or of hot or cold,
Of kind or cruel, are but heart and sense
Waging internal war.   She is the child
Of one who suffer'd here, upon the block,
Not many paces off.   The queen is kind.

BABINGTON (*proudly*).

How can I grovel in the dust to one
Whose death I planned?—of whom but some days
    past
Had I but heard she ceased to live and breathe
I had flung up my cap and shouted thus,
" Long live Queen Mary !"

ALICE (*alarmed*).

Nay, nay ! not so loud !
See, here are, roughly scrawl'd, some few poor words,
Written by one who surely is no scholar,
But one who'd die to save you.   Set your name
Here at the end.

[BABINGTON *makes a movement meaning refusal.*

Will you be merciless
Even to *friends?*   Then Heaven help your foes,
So you had pow'r to harm them !

BABINGTON.

Let me read.

[*Reads the paper which is handed to him by* ALICE.

* "Most gracious Sovereign,—If either bitter traces, or

---

* This is the original letter of Anthony Babington, though it is only to
satisfy the exigencies of the Drama that he is made to sign it at the
eleventh hour.

pensive contrite heart, and doleful sighs of a wretched
sinner, might work any pity in your royal breast, I
would wring out from my drained eyes as much
blood as, in bewraying my dreary tragedy, should
lament my fall, and somewhat, no doubt, move you
to compassion ; but since there is no proportion
between the quality of my crime and any humane
consideration, show, sweet queen, some miracle on
a wretch that lieth prostrate in your prison most
grievously bewailing his offence——" [*To* ALICE.]
Nay, do not say, "most grievously bewailing." Is
not bewailing ample ?

ALICE.

Let it stand,
" Most grievously bewailing his offence."

BABINGTON (*continuing to read*).
"and imploring such comfort at your anointed hands
——" [*To* ALICE.] "Anointed," nay, "anointed"
shall not stand. The queen is excommunicate !

ALICE.

Remember
That she was crown'd and christen'd in your faith ;
Nay, some do say it still lurks in her heart.

BABINGTON (*continuing to read*).

"as my poor wife's misfortune doth beg, my child's innocency doth crave, my guiltless family doth wish, and my heinous treachery least deserves. So shall your divine mercy make your glory shine far above all princes, as my most horrible practices are most detestable amongst your best subjects; with whom that you may long live and happily govern, I beseech the Mercy-Master to grant for His sweet Son's sake. —Your majesty's unfortunate, because disloyal, subject."

ALICE.

And now your signature.

GAOLER (*entering, having heard a shout*).

What was that shout I heard anon? It sounded strangely like sedition. Moreover, some of the other gentlemen hearing it, have taken up the cry. Rest content, sir, with the evil you have wrought, and let us have no rioting here. Why, the Tower is full of them that have followed your evil counsel! They are coming to us from all parts of England for a lodging.

M

ALICE.

Good master, this is no new sedition; 'tis but a paper asking the queen's pardon. This gentleman desires that he may sign it.

GAOLER.

He may sign it, so it is afterwards seen by those in authority.

ALICE.

Oh, it is as open as the day, the whole world may see it.

BABINGTON.

Alice, you master me, give me the paper; though 'tis but as a last straw to a drowning man.

GAOLER.

Two other gentlemen have written their confessions.

BABINGTON (*taking the pen*).

See then the force of ensample, and how men will follow one after another like a flock of sheep making for a gap in the hedge. I sign, but as I sign I know I am a dead man. Nay, I sign with all the recklessness of one that is dead already. [*Signs the paper.*

GAOLER.

Mistress, the time is up, and you remember
'Twas only by a great and special grace
You talked with Mr. Babington.

ALICE (*sadly*).

I know it,
And thank the pow'rs that be for such good grace.
God bless you, Anthony!

BABINGTON.

God bless you, Alice!
When sick men bless they say their words come true.
I am one privileged by fate to count
E'en as a sick man very nigh to death.—
From this dim border-land I spread my hands
Towards the woman that was never mine,
And say "God bless her!" as a dead man speaks,
Pale, passionless, the red blood in his veins
Frozen to stagnant ice ; God gives me grace
To pray He bless you, e'en if with another,
Some worthier man than I. Once more, farewell!

[ALICE *slowly leaves the prison, in
tears, her hands covering her face.*

M 2

SCENE II.—*The' gates of Greenwich Park.—Citizens,*
children, peasants, &c., lingering near.

[*Later in the day.*

1ST BYSTANDER.

The queen is coming. I can hear the music. I
have seen many things, but never the queen.

2ND BYSTANDER.

Then it is not the queen, since we hear she will
have no music to-day. She is altogether as sorry
for the executing of these jail-birds as she was for the
death of that pretty French gentleman, her last
husband that was to be.

3RD BYSTANDER.

Nay, they say had he been prettier the queen had
been sorrier. He was not pretty enough.

1ST BYSTANDER.

These young gentlemen are all well-favoured. As
they have gone to and fro the Hall at Westminster,
I have got so to know their features that I have almost
forgotten their heresies. I had as lief not know one
that is doomed—my heart goeth out somehow, to
one that I know.

2ND BYSTANDER.

Did you hear of the speech of Sir Christopher Hatton, and what he said of the priests and the seminaries? Sir Christopher hath a tongue in his head.

1ST BYSTANDER.

Oh, you will not work on me to say that they were in the right now. Let us rather hope they were the blackest traitors! Aye, aye, let us damn them in the next world, now that we cannot save them in this!

2ND BYSTANDER.

The Queen of Scots will never reign over us now.

1ST BYSTANDER.

Some say neither will her son.

2ND BYSTANDER (*to* 1ST).

What manner of man is the King of Scots, you that have seen him in his own land?

1ST BYSTANDER (*archly*).

Hast ever heard of Signor Davie Rizzio?

2ND BYSTANDER.

Oh ah! I see your drift! But 'tis his mother gives him his claim.

1ST BYSTANDER.

I question not his claim.   Know you that Davie
had a brother Joseph ?

2ND BYSTANDER.

Better had David borne him more like Joseph !

1ST BYSTANDER.

Nay, nay, no play on words !   This Joseph Rizzio,
Sometime a servant of the Duke of Orkney,
Told me the King of Scots was like his brother.

3RD BYSTANDER.

Well, well, the Queen of Scots was frighten'd for him,
And so her child turn'd like him.

1ST BYSTANDER.

                                        May my wife
Be never frighten'd for a base Italian
With bandy legs !   [*Hubbub and shouts in distance.*

3RD BYSTANDER.

                                Why, neighbour, thou wert right,
The queen is coming.

1ST BYSTANDER.

What ! is that the queen ?   Her head is much less

comely than those that are jingling in my pockets.
I had thought her younger.

3RD BYSTANDER.

She hath great dignity of carriage nevertheless.

2ND BYSTANDER.

Her age telleth on her.

1ST BYSTANDER.

She is, peradventure, grieving for the traitors.

3RD BYSTANDER.

But who is to rule us at her death?

1ST BYSTANDER.

Oh, the Great Turk for aught I know, with his
alcoran.   Off with your hat !

[*Enter* ALICE, *accompanied by* BABINGTON'S *wife,
and his child, which she leads by the hand, and*
WILLOUGHBY.]

WILLOUGHBY.

Make way, my good masters—these ladies wish
to get hearing of her majesty.   This is the third
day we wait her coming, failing an audience, which

is always either denied to us, or we are put off
with the cry of " to-morrow."

> [*They take up their position*
> *amongst the first row of people.*

[*Enter* ELIZABETH, *accompanied by ladies, courtiers,*
CECIL, WALSINGHAM, &c. &c.]

ELIZABETH (*hearing distant shouts*).
Why shout those blockheads, as in exultation ?

CECIL.
They shout because we overcome a foe.
Because a many-jointed snake in the grass
Is crush'd beneath your majesty's firm heel,
As erst the dragon by our own St. George—
And hence they shout.

ELIZABETH.
Nay, weep with poor St. George,
For living in a land so rife with dragons !
Where may another lurk, all crouched to spring?

ALICE (*advancing suddenly*).
My most dread sov'reign, deign to read this letter.

A COURTIER (*starting*).
Why, girl, you fling upon her majesty,

Dropping from nowhere, you astonish us.

Not thus the fashion to approach a queen.

Give first your letter to some officer.

Hast heard of mediators ?   A high prince

Takes nothing thus raw-handed from the clutch

Of such a sudden apparition ! [*Aside.*]   Zounds !

Why, had she been the Pope or Antichrist,

She had not scared me more !   The girl is comely.

This comes of Cecil's foolish hurlyburlies

Of jointed snakes and dragons ! [*To* ALICE.]   Say

  your business ?

ELIZABETH.

What is it ?   Nay, I guess before I see !

COURTIER.

Your majesty's keen sense dives down the well,

Unearthing squeamish truth, who hides her head, ·

Like your old ostrich that has eaten nails,

And deems the world too blind to make a note

Of her tail feathers !

ELIZABETH.

   Ha !   Well said, well said !

Tho', like your ostrich, somewhat long of limb

And scant of feathers !   Now your business, girl—

That well-thumbed paper in your pretty hand
(The girl is pretty) is a supplication
For pardon of these Catholics?

ALICE.

It is,

My most dread sov'reign! Foremost is my pray'r
For Mr. Babington. This is his child !

[*Thrusting forward the child.*

ELIZABETH.

A pretty boy.

COURTIER (*aside*).

Why is it that the spawn

Of traitors, like the slimy eggs of serpents,
Ever accumulates and multiplies,
Whilst God's anointed—the high princes of earth,
Go virgin, or are barren, or give birth
To one poor addled egg? [*Aloud.*] A pretty boy.

ALICE (*continuing*).

Ah, madam ! let your merciful renown
Spread over sea, to far-off continents !
Let him be foremost of an embassage
To blow the clarions sounding forth your praise

O'er that new land discover'd in the west—
But only let him live, tho' far away,
To bless your name !　　　[*Kneels to the Queen.*

ELIZABETH (*compassionately*).
　　　　　You are his wife, poor girl.
See, Walsingham, this is a traitor's wife—
A traitor "art and part," are those the words ?
A traitor found red-handed in the fact,
Yet not so very terrible, what say you ?

WALSINGHAM (*coldly*).
She hath the pity of the realm with mine——

ELIZABETH.
Which serves her little.　Add our own thereto,
How will it serve her ?

ALICE (*imploringly*).
　　　　　Madam, add to this
One little stroke of your anointed hand.
Give him at least his life, he is so young !

ELIZABETH (*affected*).
Thou art a right good pleader.

WALSINGHAM (*sternly*).
　　　　　Hark you, madam,

I pity this poor lady, ne'ertheless
This man must die.

CECIL.

To spare him is to spare
The other Papists that are doom'd to death.
He is the ringleader, the law demands
Her lord shall die ! We spare not such as he.

ELIZABETH.

Go to, my lord ! we follow our own bent,
And spare or spare not, as it seems us good.   .
Preach you unto some other, not the Queen !
God's mercy, sirs !

ALICE.

Ah, he is not my lord,
He is my cousin only and my friend.
This lady is his wife.   [*Pointing to* MRS. BABINGTON.

ELIZABETH.

Alas, poor lady !

CECIL (*to* MRS. BABINGTON).
You, madam, being wedded to a traitor,
One that was sworn to compass the queen's death,
Should bear such sorrow silently.   Time was

When traitors' wives did perish with their husbands,
And time may be again, it being known
They do consort with them and keep their company—
And those that keep the company of traitors
Cannot go unsuspected.   Be content
To know you do not die with Mr. Babington.

MRS. BABINGTON.

-Would I could die with him, my dear, dear husband !
[*Covers her face and weeps.   Recovering herself.*
This, his good cousin, who hath hitherto
Spoken for my cause only, needs a word—
For her own flesh and blood, one Jerome Bellamy,
Is likewise of the number doom'd to die.
He is no ringleader, and only suffers
For having known the rest and harbour'd them.
Methinks I am as treasonable as he.

WALSINGHAM.

Said I not so ?   To spare this Babington
Will be to spare a whole hot-bed of traitors !

ELIZABETH.

'Tis over late to plead.   We will consider.

ALICE.

We strove to reach your grace's ear before,
Yet were denied.

WILLOUGHBY (*leading* ALICE *away from the* QUEEN).
Ah, cousin, we have done !
We can but vex by importunity.
Pray heaven we be not now too late to plead !
Yet if we be, and you left desolate,
Remember what I have of home is yours.
My mother will be mother too to you.
I say this come what may.

ALICE (*weeping*).
Say it not now—
It is too soon !

WILLOUGHBY.
Yet did I wait till after
I could not speak. Your heart, new-wrung with grief,
Would harden to me, so I say my say ;
Nor hope for aught save that you have the grace
To grant my boon by taking what small good
I have to offer.

ALICE.
You are passing kind
Good cousin. I deserve and hope for nothing.

WILLOUGHBY.
There is an inner mid-heart sanctuary,

Whereof the walls are stouter than the Tower's,
Built danger-proof, love's holiest of holies,
And you have enter'd there.   Remember this.

ALICE.

I do remember, and I thank you for it.
God grant the queen will show her mercy to us !

[*Sounds of artillery heard in the distance mingled with
the ringing of bells.*]

ELIZABETH (*listening*).
What means yon booming thunder ?

WALSINGHAM (*advancing*).
It means that now, at this hour, the conspiracy
directed against the person of your most sacred
majesty is at an end, and that John Ballard, Anthony
Babington, John Savage, Robert Barnwell, Chidiock
Titchborne, Charles Tilney, and Edward Abington,
after having been drawn on hurdles from the Tower
to the place of their suffering in St. Giles's Fields,
have been hanged and quartered while they were yet
quick.   So perish all the enemies of the queen !

[MRS. BABINGTON *faints* ;
WILLOUGHBY *supports her*.

QUEEN (*shuddering*).
Oh, horrible ! this shall not be again !

CECIL, WALSINGHAM, and COURTIERS.
So perish all the queen's enemies !

VOICES OF THE PEOPLE.
God save the queen !

[*Men pass amongst the people carrying trays with flagons*
of ale, wine, &c.]

A CITIZEN (*to* WILLOUGHBY).
Come, drink a glass with us, good citizen !   Here's
to the oversetting of our foes.

WILLOUGHBY.
I cannot drink ; methinks the drink would choke
me.   Make way for these ladies.
[*Endeavouring to pass out of crowd.*

CITIZEN.
Oh, it is not a strong liquor—none of your Spanish
heresies.   But, maybe, you are a Papist ?

WILLOUGHBY.
Nay, give me a glass then.   [*Drinks.*]   Yea, so

perish all the queen's enemies! Yet, my good sirs, if I drink not this toast with altogether a cheerful countenance, it is that these ladies knew some of these gentlemen. Some of them just done to death had been known to them for many years, nay, I knew them myself, also; therefore I will say—So perish all the enemies of the queen's majesty! But God grant that amongst them there be none of our own true friends!

[*Curtain falls.*]

EPILOGUE.

Back to the common things of ev'ry day—
  The dull prosaic Present with its cares !—
The curtain falls on this imperfect play,
  The actors reassume what dress was theirs
Ere yet they donned the doublet and trunk hose
  Of good Queen Bess's reign! We live once more
In days that seem too far removed from those
  Bright days of chivalry, when patriots swore
Rash oaths for what they deemed their country's good,
  Fired by a faith our placid souls ignore.
Where are the eager pulsings of the blood,
  Those noble aspirations, which of yore
Banded together to some futile end,   ˙
  The flower of English youth, who dared disgrace
And cruel death, and perish'd friend with friend,
  In their fresh years of manhood ? Nay !—(efface
From out your minds the thought, or else extol
  Our growing wealth and commerce in its stead)—
Gone are those high ambitions of the soul !
  The golden days of chivalry are dead !
          *   *   *   *   *
Thus have I heard some Englishmen lament,
  Who deemed themselves elected to declaim
Against the Present, with the discontent
  Of souls appointed to despise and blame.

Yet 'tis but just these favoured few should say
   (Betwixt their carping) : 'Neath a peaceful reign
We dwell and draw our breath, nor dread to-day
   Fall'n France, staunch Scotland, or disjointed Spain ;
For us no ghastly scaffold draped in black,
   Uprises like a spectre to affright ;
Whilst halter, hurdle, quart'ring-knife, and rack
   Have languish'd under liberty and light,
Till thought of them is as of clouds that lower
   After the night is past when storms have been,
That cede to sun.   And I have seen the Tow'r,
   (Guest of a guardsman of sweet seventeen,
Who asked me there to tea,) yet smiled beneath
   That gloomy pile, as heedless of their fate
Who once, predestin'd to a horrid death,
   Defiled despairing, through the Traitors' Gate.
Nor did my pulses falter as I turn'd
   From time to time to view with bated breath
Some record of bold spirits that had burn'd
   Their moth-wings at the altar of their faith.
He, smoking carelessly the while, forgot
   The brave Sir Walter, with his outspread cloak
Before the Virgin Queen, whose name should not
   Go unremember'd of the ones who smoke
The fragrant weed that comforts their curl'd heads
   (The which he brought us ere he left his own
Some few short paces hence).   And yet he treads—
   That beardless warrior, who hath never known,
As yet, the taste of blood, the clash of arms—
   As though these names said nothing to his soul.
Yes, gone their vain ambitions, their alarms
   Still'd with those legions that, as ages roll,

Are garner'd 'neath the sweeping scythe of Time,
  Leaving us transient sojourners to mark
Some graven coat-of-arms, or pious rhyme
  Such as I mark'd that day ! Yet tho' so dark
The blot that fell their coat-of-arms upon
  Who swore to kill the queen in days of yore
(When Titchborne, Tilney, Ballard, Babington,
  Like kites transfix'd against a granary door,
Suffer'd to scare their fellows), who may say
  What these had wrought beneath a brighter star ?
Or what deserving impulse turn'd astray
  Divides the thing we were from what we are ?
Then let us honour what they counted good,
  Nor blame the zeal we may not understand ;
Nor, loathing, shrink from names that might have stood
  As high as any in our English land,
For worth and courage hitherto unstain'd,
  These hang their heads, and suppliant, meet our view,
Before the bar of history arraigned,
  And asking pity, win our pardon too.
Yet bless these days if men have learnt at last,
  The good of nations makes the good of kings ;
Whilst Ignorance and Bigotry "are cast,
  As weeds, upon the dunghill of dead things." *

* " Songs before Sunrise," p. 24.

—